D1599843

PRAISE FOR *ONLY 10s 2.0*

"*Only 10s 2.0* is a clear, workable system for us all. It brings a new way of seeing our to-do lists. I use it with all my CEO clients because it works immediately and it sticks with them. If you are feeling overwhelmed or you are an overachiever, you will be forever changed by reading it."

Helen Appleby, Executive Coach and Author of *The Unwritten Rules of Women's Leadership*

"What I love about Mark's book, *Only 10s 2.0*, is that it gives a very human and personal account of his own journey from discovering he had A.D.D to creating a bespoke system that has helped him and tens of thousands of high achievers overcome dropping balls, procrastination, and fear of letting people down. If you have a brilliantly sharp mind where ideas dance around like a moth near a lightbulb, or if you find it hard to prioritize and focus your time and attention on things that really matter, then read this book. It will help you create an extraordinary life you love leading."

David Foster, Master Coach and Author of *Where's Dad?*

"Only *10s 2.0* cleverly uses your to-do list to break you out of the prison cell of your own making.

Jason Goldberg, Transformational Speaker and Author of *Prison Break*

"If time is the greatest commodity we have in life, and I very much believe it is, Only *10s 2.0* sets us up to make the most of ours. Learning to have difficult conversations and take ownership over the way we allocate our precious minutes isn't just for CEO's and entrepreneurs, it's for all of us. This book is a gem."

Stephen Kellogg, Musician, Speaker, and Author of *Objects in the Mirror.*

"*Only 10s 2.0* is a fantastic, helpful resource for any executive, entrepreneur, or business leader looking to elevate their performance and achievement."

Alan Stein, Author of *Raise Your Game*

"*Only 10s 2.0* takes the reader on a journey of self-exploration into what's most important in your life and business. This book goes beyond the simple to-do list and has the reader confront where in their life they have unconsciously rendered themselves powerless to their busyness. I loved the first edition of this book and the new content that 2.0 delivers take this masterpiece to another level. If you want to up level your relationship to your work, your schedule and yourself *Only 10s 2.0* will be game changer for you."

Devon Bandison, The Game Changer Coach and Author of *Fatherhood is Leadership*

"*Only 10s 2.0* is a lifesaver for anyone looking to become more efficient and effective. That's all of us, right? In this program, Mark has created a simple, yet profound tool for productivity. The inspiring and entertaining storytelling also contained in this book is a bonus!"

Brady Sadler, Entrepreneur, Co-founder of Double Elvis
Productions, and Author of *Collaboration is King*

"Mark's *Only 10s* workshop with my team has been game-changing. He is able to merge high-level behavioral awareness and powerful, practical tools in a way that has allowed us to take ownership of our time and life, both personally, and professionally. *2.0* goes even deeper and will be on my desk at all times. Highly recommended."

Teo Alfero, Teacher, author of *The Wolf Connection*,
What Wolves Can Teach Us About Being Human,
and CEO/Founder of Wolf Connection.

"*Only 10s 2.0* is turbo-charged with even more depth and breadth of hard truths and practical guidance on why and how to turn our to do lists into the guiding lights to a happier, more fulfilled life. It's a must read and a must re-read for anyone that's trying to make better choices."

Chris Colbert, Speaker, Innovator, Author of *This is It*,
Former Managing Director, Harvard Innovation Labs
and host of the Insert Human Podcast

"*Only 10s* is a transformational life management system masquerading as a time and attention management tool. It's a powerful (and uncomfortable) reminder that most of us don't have a time management problem at all. We have an honesty problem…and a focus problem…and a boundaries problem… and a willingness to speak up problem. So often we aren't taking responsibility for everything that's happening in our lives — we choose to believe that we are a victim of circumstance instead of the owner of our life. *Only 10s* is a wake-up call to get honest with ourselves and those around us. To do the deep self-inquiry and self-reflection that will help us live more intentionally, focused on what matters most to us (The 10s)."

Shelley Paxton, Speaker, Transformational Coach, Author of
Soulbbatical A Corporate Rebel's Guide to Finding Your Best Life
and host of the Rebel Souls Podcast.

PRAISE FOR *ONLY 10s*

"Silverman's stories are moving and his life solutions are innovative and powerful. I highly recommend this book!!!"

Steve Chandler, Author of *Crazy Good*

"Mark Silverman is gifted with bottom-line honesty, which shines through this short but potent book. If you can grasp even a portion of Mark's sense of pointed intention, you will be well ahead of where you stood before. Mark is devoted to living at the frequency of purpose, and he would love to have you meet him there. Don't hesitate to fly."

Alan Cohen, Author of *A Deep Breath of Life*

"Mark is first and foremost an incredible human being, friend, and a dedicated coach; he's highly intentional and he makes things happen when he says he will – for himself and for others. And as he points out in this new book, he's also learned the fine art of prioritization. It's the key to making the most important things happen in your life. If it's not a "hell yes" for now, then it's a "hell no." As you learn to slow down and trust your gut, you too will be able to sift the 10s out of the pile – jettison the rest – and watch your productivity and fulfillment soar. Mark outlines the techniques he uses which have been proven to work for him; give them a try and thrive!"

Kelli Richards, CEO, All Access Group

"Mark's idea of living life by following only your 10 out of 10s is a game changer. It transcends the latest fads in time-management, online scheduling or planning apps. It also moves beyond complex systems like David Allen's Getting Things Done or Steven Covey's Four Quadrants. Warren Buffett once said, "The difference between successful people and really successful people is that really successful people say no to almost everything." The only problem is how do you know what to say no to? If you are overwhelmed by never-ending to-do lists, *Only 10s* will help you cut straight to the heart of time and life management. And it gives you a road map for when to say Hell Yes and when to say Hell No. *Only 10s* is a must read for entrepreneurs, executives, leaders, and innovators."

Rich Litvin, Co-author of *The Prosperous Coach*
and Founder of 4PC

Author photo: Vadym Guliuk

YOU DON'T HAVE A TIME MANAGEMENT PROBLEM,
YOU HAVE AN HONESTY PROBLEM.

ONLY 10s 2.0

☑ CONFRONT YOUR TO-DO LIST
☑ TRANSFORM YOUR LIFE

MARK J. SILVERMAN

Host of the Mastering Midlife podcast

DEDICATION

John, Jake, Zack, Savannah, Robin,
Marla, Kevin, Brady, Darian,
and those on the way…You are my heart.

TABLE OF CONTENTS

PREFACE

WALKING THE WALK

It isn't always easy to admit it, but back in 2015, I couldn't see what a revelation *Only 10s* was. I can see now that I've spent too much time downplaying its impact, clarity, and transformative power.

I wrote *Only 10s* for an audience of one … me. Truth be told -- I didn't think anyone would really read it. Yet I published *Only 10s*, and 1500 copies went the first day. The same number sold on the second day. A total of 10,000 copies in the first week. People posted positive reviews and sent messages about what a game changer it was for them. Some well-known authors wrote testimonials. Other coaches gave it to their CEO clients to inspire them to focus. Even my mentor acknowledged the book was something special. Inside though, I was asking myself why?

The book was rushed, I thought. I hadn't understood the need for copy editing, after all. It was written Fire, Ready, Aim. I knew it went public with its weak grammar and misspellings. But still, tens of thousands of copies of my personal PhD program made their way around the world.

I wasn't in a place to allow myself to accept the praise. I only saw the typos and poor writing. It came from me, and I discounted the 10,000 hours of reading, learning, and workshops prior to it, and I knew that the concepts weren't new or all that unique. I diminished

Only 10s. Yet, I'd taught the workshops and seen the lightbulbs go on. I didn't know how to build a polished machine like David Allen and his overwhelming (to me) Getting Things Done industry, so *Only 10s* got no respect from ... me.

Then I re-read it a few years later, and I was reminded that I never had a time management problem. I had an honesty problem.

Apparently it wasn't just me that had an honesty problem! So many people sent me messages saying it was like I had written the book for them.

Once the rights to the book reverted to me, my assistant Gayle Bu took it upon herself to re-edit the book. She is incredibly competent, and a perfectionist, so in her hands the book uplevelled beautifully. She corrected the grammar and misspellings.

As I re-read it after Gayle worked her magic, I found myself wondering who had written that insightful chapter on fear. I asked myself who came up with the great toolbox? It was like I was reading another person's work. It was that good. The book resonated with me just like it had been written *for* me. It was simple, direct, kind, and unflinching in its mission to get the reader (me) to take responsibility for everything in their (my) life.

If you believe in the muse --- that mystical entity that creates music, paints paintings, and yes, writes books, then you will understand that I could not simply *write **Only 10s**.* I needed to bring it into the world for myself first. It was written *through* me and *for* me. The good news is that no matter what I believed, thousands have benefitted.

So from here on in, I will take credit for the book with my name on it. We will know where it really came from, but with a wink. ;)

What I created as an exercise in time management and motivation for myself and to benefit my clients, workshop attendees, and those who came across the book organically, turned into a multi-year journey of self-discovery. I didn't just write *Only*

10s, I practiced it too and because I practiced it, I knew it worked. By analyzing my to-do list and critically asking why things were on it — read as, figuring out where I was lying to myself — I discovered my fears and distractions were hidden in the list itself. I improved relationships and moved so much off my plate that I felt free to create. For the first time in my life I was getting things done. I was having tough conversations that were really honest. If it wasn't a *10* for me, well then, I'd let it go. Blame it on *Only 10s*.

Then something happened.

I'd seen a lot of personal success with my productivity. Professionally the book and the *Only 10s* workshops were selling steadily. At some point though, I'd stopped writing everything on my white board. On occasion when I did use the board, it was without the level of commitment I'd had before. It became a *10*-if-I-feel-like-it board, and a I'll-get-to-it-tomorrow board. Important things dropped out. The habit had only lasted while it was fun.

It seemed that *Only 10s*, like anything for someone with ADD, lasted only as long as it was stimulating.

Even though the book kept selling and I continued to do workshops, and *Only 10s* was being quoted all over the place, once the newness and awesomeness of my newly-birthed system wore off, I wasn't walking the walk as well as I'd like to be able to report. But here is something I only saw recently when I decided to publish *Only 10s 2.0*: Even when I wasn't practicing the *Only 10s* system, it was still benefitting me because it had taught me to be honest with myself.

I GOT WOKE WITH ONLY *10s*.

When I got distracted, I saw it. When I said yes to a 6, I saw it. Even if what I chose was less than a *10*, or even just a distraction, I could see it as a choice. The unconscious victim could not come back. On one hand, I would let go of a *10*, using the excuse of "I'll take the consequences" but that's the beauty of it. I had chosen those consequences. Whatever my predicament, I was *choosing* to be there either through action or inaction. I saw **Only 10s** with new appreciation when I repeatedly fell off the wagon of practicing it fully. Although it felt like ten steps forward and eight steps back, those two steps (honesty and responsibility) were the first building blocks to create a lifetime of practice and growth.

And we *want* solid building blocks. We *want* our own experience. We *want* to be the captains of our own lives.

Failing honestly at **Only 10s** is not failing … it is learning.

Stop doing **Only 10s**? Recognize it. Start again. Rinse. Repeat.

The five years since I published **Only 10s** have changed me. I've had the great fortune to talk to people about the **Only 10s** concepts daily and while engaging with them I've been reminded about my own need to have difficult conversations, be honest with myself, make sure everything that is on my to-do list ought to be, eliminate expectations in favor of agreements, be clear in my communications, keep my word, and renegotiate when I am unable to.

It's entirely true: We teach what we most need to learn.

I wasn't going to learn all these skills or confront the fears and conditioning just because I put the digit 10 next to an action item. I needed to wrestle with it. Triumph and failure. And in doing so grow, expand, find clarity, and learn to celebrate the process as I journeyed along.

When I wrote **Only 10s**, I was recognizing the actions of someone who was no longer a door mat or a martyr. I learned some skills to set boundaries; not immediately, and not quickly, but gradually. It took a lot of practice, but over time I learned. I screwed up at first and then I got it right. I changed.

I feel certain that every person in my life today would describe me as direct and honest, and that they would say I am always willing to ask for what I want and to set a boundary. I had occasion to be part of a leadership training and the participants were separated into two groups. The first was made up of those judged to be the shyer more passive dudes and the second group were judged to be arrogant, defiant, alpha types … guess which group I landed in? The feedback was that I was a bad ass. That had not been me before ***Only 10s***.

In the time after I wrote ***Only 10s*** and practiced, stopped, and started with its key practices, another thing happened. I became kinder and more loving. Resentments couldn't take hold, and if they did, I knew what to do to relieve them. I realized that if I had a resentment, it was on me. I had not set a boundary, or I did not ask for what I wanted (or I was just a little jealous).

The program I created to get things done, with instructions and practices, became a way of being in the world for me.

I was a strong No! to the suggestion that I produce a second edition of *Only 10s*.

I had my reasons.

- *I get bored easily.* Reading the same book twice is pushing it for me. Re-writing the same book felt beyond my tolerance. I don't even go over my answers once more on a test if I have extra time. When I'm done, I'm done. Moving forward is my modus operandi. Revisit the same content? No thanks. Not me. Bo-ring.

- *I live for the adrenaline rush of the creative process.* Once the initial excitement is spent, so is my interest. One time I taught myself to play guitar so I could give a talk and then actually sing on a "being willing to fail" weekend. I faced my greatest fear--singing in public. I played and sang on stage and even got a standing ovation. I never picked up the guitar again. No need. Process complete. Moving on.

- *I didn't understand the book's worth.* People who read **Only 10s** told me it was "good" and that it had an impact on them. Other coaches I knew gave it to CEOs and I witnessed some of the language of **Only 10s** find its way into common speech around relationships with time. It kept selling -- tens of thousands per year. I heard all that. But I never really saw the value.

- *My language is different now.* I was a new writer when I penned **Only 10s**, learning the principles at the same time as I was crafting them to pass on to readers. After five years, I've worked the program and taught it to tens of thousands of folks. The way I address the more effective concepts is different now. I am a better writer and coach. I felt pulled to create something new to reflect my evolution (Mastering Midlife) more than I wanted to consider what still worked and needed further exploration in **Only 10s**.

Assuming there might be some strength to the idea of a second edition that I hadn't seen, I pulled a copy of **Only 10s** from the shelf, daring to challenge my unfettered instinct to declare a hard No!

I was dumbfounded by what I saw and read.

Who wrote this?

I saw the chapters on honesty, choice, and fear with fresh eyes. They blew my mind -- even though I've been teaching the concepts in workshops for years, the lessons still held true.

- The "qualifier" places every item either on or off the to-do list and is a key to how we operate in many other areas of our lives. Inquire about the qualifier and learn about you.

- I saw that getting honest with my to-do list moved me from victim of circumstances to the owner of my life (time and attention). We need to get honest about our choices.

- Whether setting a boundary, asking for what I want, saying no, or creating a clear agreement, being willing to have these sweaty-palmed, risky-feeling difficult conversations, makes the biggest impact. We need to be having more of these.

- Ten minutes of honest planning changes the trajectory of the day, the week and the rest of life. Everyone has ten minutes. Everyone.

- Two hours of deep work twice a week transforms creation. We simply have to find those hours.

Those are the tangible, operational lessons. To get to these though, the path isn't always a straight line. In my client sessions and teaching work with *Only 10s* I've heard every story that a person can tell themselves to *not* adopt the lessons of the qualifier, choose the elements of the list, plan, have the conversations and so on. To get to the tools requires first getting past the stories we tell ourselves and the shoulds, can'ts, and if-I-do-that-thens imbedded in the stories. Once reviewed I was able to nail down ten truths that I coach people on in order for them to see the full benefit of the *Only 10s* way, and I've included them here as highlights of *Only 10s 2.0*.

TEN TRUTHS OF *ONLY 10s*

Folks who have done coaching with me, attended a workshop, seen and heard me on my Facebook lives, or are guests on my podcast know my reactions to their struggles with time management well. I always name what I'm seeing when I hear clients lying to themselves to justify saying yes to things that aren't **10s** in their lives and I mirror their story right back at them:

"Ohhhhh, I get it. You can't do **Only 10s** because …"

… someone else put this on your plate and you had absolutely no say about it.

We opt into the victim role so easily. It's a habit. Exasperated and overwhelmed, clients tell me that they don't know how "it" happened, and tell me "it" is out of their control. They know better than this, (of course they do) and then they sometimes follow up with, "but what could I do?" I've seen powerful CEOs throw their hands up and say, "I just can't find the time" (to do strategic planning.) My favorite is: "they overschedule me." *They* do it to me. *They* overschedule the CEO, (everybody's boss' boss). Do they really? Really?

That's how it feels until they decide to confront the "victim" and all its implications.

I witnessed this one firsthand years ago and because it could have had horrible personal outcomes for me, it has really stuck. I vividly remember sitting in a hospital bed with my leg marked up for surgery. My Achilles tendon had cried uncle. I was waiting for my turn to be wheeled into the operating suite. My doctor rushed in. She looked tired, distracted, and a bit disheveled. I had chosen Dr. N because my previous foot doctor was a drunk (just my hunch), and messed up my previous surgery, redid it, and messed it up further. Dr. N was uber-competent, came highly recommended, and had been impeccably put together at all of our appointments, but that day she looked like crap. It was 11:30 a.m. and I had been scheduled for 10 a.m.

"You ready, Mark?"

"Yup ...You okay?"

She sighed and replied, "Yes, I've already done four procedures and I'm behind. I'm so sorry. I have six after you. I haven't even eaten. My team overschedules me every surgery day." I'd heard her say that before in the office when she was running behind.

Alarm bells went off in my brain. I'd already had two botched surgeries. I said, "You know what, I'm fine here. Why don't you go grab something to eat?"

She looked so relieved. Thirty minutes later she was back to her old self. Her energy had shifted from night to day. She thanked me. "I had a salad and a cup of coffee. I am so much better. Thank you."

I laughed and because I am so direct said, "You look better, and by the way, you weren't gonna touch my foot the way you looked this morning." (I sure hope I'm as charming as I think I am.)

"Yeah, I don't blame you ... I really should tell them, but they always squeeze more people in."

I am not confident that conversation ever happened.

I'd been there in my work life before and I never knew I had a choice when someone else put something on my plate. I thought it was now mine to deal with since it was on my plate. It never occurred to me that I had any say. The result of not knowing that I could do anything about it was steadily growing resentment of my work and my colleagues.

Only 10s changed all that. I saw the lie and I could never unsee it after. I was afraid to say no. I didn't have the sense of self-worth, the self-esteem, or self-respect to say a simple no.

WE DON'T HAVE A TIME MANAGEMENT PROBLEM, WE HAVE AN HONESTY PROBLEM.

"Ohhhhh, I get it. You can't do *Only 10s* because …"

… you consider being "so busy" a badge of honor.

"Man, what a day! I couldn't catch my breath once," my clients say, as if playing the victim card is automatic qualification for the hero medal or the badge of honor for being overwhelmed. Doesn't it feel good, that all you can do is crawl into the house, crack open a beer or pour a glass of wine and be exhausted from all your hard work? You now have the justification to complain, to veg out and watch your TV shows, be grumpy, and not engage with your family. You work so hard, after all, right?

I'm not very proud to admit it, but I relished in this at one time, covering up that I just didn't have the courage or the sense of self-worth to set a freaking boundary. I was too afraid to look weak, like I couldn't handle it all, or what was worse for me, face the disdain of whoever my oppressor was. By not wanting to appear weak … I hope you are ahead of me here … I was actually, in reality, truly … being weak. Nauseating. Ick.

And isn't it a bit of a boon to our self-worth (and a cover up for any feelings of inadequacy) to tell the world, "I just can't give any more?" What a great excuse to not tap into all that unrealized potential (that you know you have waiting inside of you). Hint: resistance is rearing its ugly head again. The purpose of this victim mentality is to keep you from realizing what you could create, what you have always wanted to create, "if I only had the time."

YOU'RE TOO BUSY BECAUSE IT FEELS EASIER THAN CHOOSING WHAT IS IMPORTANT.

"Ohhhhh, I get it. You can't do *Only 10s* because …"

… you can't possibly delegate that.

You stare at your to-do list. There isn't one single item that could possibly be delegated. Everything needs to be yours, doesn't it? This one feels sticky, like it isn't going to be possible to overcome for some people. Some folks get it right away and start handing things off with a vengeance, and some fight it. As I work with people on *Only 10s,* it is that stickiness we are interested in. It is in the stickiness where the gold lies. So when you run into a wall, rejoice. You found a golden key. If you don't hit that wall, rejoice, you get to skip this level and are off to find YOUR keys.

If you can't find anything to delegate, awesome!

Some kind of limitation exists that you need to discard. In other words, welcome to resistance. This is the wall and you've hit it. The good news is that the door to freedom is right there, and you can go ahead and fiddle with the lock.

Here is a story that I hope will illustrate this truth for you.

Client: " Joe's people jump when he asks. They do the work, bring back quality product, and he doesn't have to lift a finger. I wish my team would do that. Instead, I am constantly doing things myself because they regularly miss deadlines, or if they do something I delegate to them, it comes back in such bad shape that I have to spend the night fixing it."

Me: "How did Joe create his team that way, and how did YOU create your team the way it is?"

Client: "Joe doesn't accept shoddy work or excuses. But people don't like him."

Me: "Do they respect him?"

Client: "Of course they do ... And actually, they'd fall on a sword for him."

Me: [Silent]

Client: "I get it, I want to be liked. I worry about them being overwhelmed. I wonder what they would think I actually do."

Me: "What else?"

Client: "Shit ... and I don't send the work back. I don't train them to do it better. I don't hold anyone accountable because I want them to like me. I want to be part of the team instead of the leader of the team."

So, an item needs to be delegated. What is the thought or feeling you're having about that? Lean into it.

Tightness in your chest? A headache? Fear? What is that voice in your head saying?

"They're already overworked."

"They will think I'm not one of the team."

"I am the only one who can do it right."

"They'll screw it up."

"I'll just have to redo it."

"If they do it, what will I do?" (This is a hidden gem of many senior leaders.)

You will need to confront the self-talk and lies your brain tells you to stop you from delegating. It's not easy, but you can't reach the heights you're aiming for without letting go of some of the baggage.

IF YOU'RE OVERWHELMED, YOU ARE PROBABLY DOING SOMEONE ELSE'S JOB.

"Ohhhhh, I get it. You can't do *Only 10s* because …"

… only doing *10s* will ruin your relationships.

It will. If by "ruin" you mean change, and by relationships, you mean those interactions you have with others who depend on you to twist yourself into a pretzel for them all the time, then yes, change is coming. Relationships are agreements, spoken and unspoken. When you change the rules, you change the relationship. Those who need you to stay in the box of who you were, will have trouble continuing to support the person you are becoming. Those who support you to grow and reach your potential, will shift with you. What you'll be left with is an authentic community of supportive teammates, responsive to one another's wants and needs and … boundaries. The road to building this community will be bumpy, but it is definitely worth travelling.

My ex-wife Robin often said, "when you walk into a room, 50% of the people will like you and 50% won't … except Mark … 100% of them will like Mark." And this was completely by design.

If you're like me at all, you went through life people pleasing -- taking on stress so others would not need to, deferring to others … all to avoid conflict. With *Only 10s* you *will* have an abrupt change in experience. Once you grow knees and elbows and actually take up space in the world, your world changes. The conflict you have been carefully avoiding comes home to roost. It can be subtle or vicious.

I learned that when I take up space, the world pushes back. But build that muscle, allow your nervous system to adapt to this new experience, and I promise, it will be worth it.

I had a client who was a brilliant entrepreneur. Business ideas poured out of him in every conversation. But he was struggling to get traction. He was married with kids, loved his wife, had an infectious personality, and was a pleasure to be around. When I started poking around his life to find clues to his financial challenges, a picture emerged. He lived in a big house which also included his wife's parents and his chronically unemployed brother. Other than cooking meals, the parents contributed nothing, and the brother watched a lot of TV. Top this off with the entire crew including his wife, who did love him, constantly criticizing him. So now, given your objective vantage point, you know exactly what needed to happen: boundaries. People needed to be kicked out. Conversations needed to take place. But in his own family, our hero had been trained when he was a child that he had no rights. You get what you get and do not ask for more. He learned to avoid conflict with his narcissistic mother and absent father at all costs and it was his job to care for everyone. It was his identity. His purpose and reason for being. It was also the reason everyone loved him in the outside world. A gift and a curse.

After some time working together on this, he began to see the oppression for himself and he knew what needed to happen. He recognized that conversations needed to be had. He had no idea "how" he was going to do it, or if he could, which is what obscured the solution in the first place (more on that later), but he did see the path out.

So, we created a plan. Baby steps. Step one: enroll his wife in a new way of treating him. They were in couples therapy, so they had a platform to work on this. Step two: she becomes his ally in the family. Step three, four, and five: Set boundaries with the family and shuffle living situations.

People got pissed. He was called selfish, greedy, and unloving -- at first -- but after months of holding his ground, and loving himself, his world began to re-order. And this shift in relationships is what gave him the space to focus on his business. His ability to set boundaries gave him the confidence to make asks of his community that could grow revenue.

None of this was easy or pleasant. But, if you ask him (and his wife) … it has all been worth it. The bonus? His shift changed the legacy he will leave for his kids forever.

ONCE YOU START TO TAKE UP SPACE, PEOPLE RESPOND, AND YOUR WORLD CHANGES.

"Ohhhhh, I get it. You can't do *Only 10s* because …"

… if you only do *10s*, you'll have to drop something important.

In every workshop someone blurts out," what if I miss something important?" I watch as panic sets in for the self-proclaimed expert plate spinner. I don't fix their panic immediately.

"Oh, you *will* drop things out," I say, waiting while they absorb that I'm not letting them off the hook. "But tell the truth … didn't you drop things out before? How many things spun off those plates you are desperately turning already … and weren't many of them important? Maybe even *10s*?"

People always know this to be true, but that doesn't make them feel any better.

The 4s, 5s, and 6s have gotta go. They are the weeds choking the plant. They are easy to see, and it starts to make sense to just whack them off the list as you move through the process. But 7s and 8s are wiley MFers. They pretend to be *10s*. They could be important. You could have some juice around them. You will need to make a conscious, difficult, and deliberate choice and pull them out by the root for the *10*. Look at this another way. Instead of pulling weeds you are pruning a tree. The more you trim, the stronger the limbs that remain, and the more you have say over the shape the tree grows as it reaches for the sky. The 9s are the killers. They have value; they are tied to relationships; there are consequences to not keeping them on the list, and often the *10* is dealing with those consequences. But 9s somehow never get done. There are always issues with 9s. Resistance, things going wrong, too many resources are required. Yet 9s will suck the life out of you so ridding yourself of a 9 is rocket fuel. If something is a 7, 8, or 9, it probably wasn't going to get done … unless you were using it to avoid your **10** (but that's for a later discussion). You weren't committed. If you did get it done, you were left with the feeling of not accomplishing anything that day … because you were distracted by that 7, 8, or 9. It's true, you can always do them. Any of them. They just don't belong on your list and you could do them AFTER your **10s**. Which is also when you can lose yourself in Twitter or Netflix and chill, or meditate on the nature of the universe. Or scoop up a 4, a 7, or find out a 9 was a **10** all along, and do that.

YOU HAVE TO TRUST THAT IF IT WANTS TO BE A 10, IT WILL COME BACK AROUND AND MAKE ITSELF A 10 EVERY TIME.

"Ohhhhh, I get it. You can't do **Only 10s** because …"

… people will think you're lazy or call you selfish.

You do know you don't really exist, right? What other people think of you is 95%, actually 100%, projection of their own thoughts (but that's for my next book), feelings and conditioning. Remember back to the fourth truth where you were worried about ruining relationships? Where you were caring so much about those people who depended on you that you stayed squarely in your box? Yes, those who cannot set a boundary, will think you are lazy, and selfish, and (gasp!) say you're not a team player. They have to, because they cannot do for themselves what you are doing for you. It is the first law of projection, "criticize those doing what I secretly wish I could do but wouldn't dare." The reason it bothers you is that it plays into your own inner critic. If it didn't, it wouldn't bother you. Still, it takes fortitude to not take on those projections. It is another muscle to build. The secret ingredient to the rocket fuel you are craving is cultivating that focus. Most people can't do it and also criticize those who do.

P.S. More often than not, nobody is thinking of you at all. It's you that thinks you're lazy. Either way, avoid the trap.

Stephanie was 29 when she got promoted to VP at her corporate finance position. As a supervisor, she had hands-on work as well as leadership duties. She was still close enough to the team that she felt part of it as a supervisor, but with her promotion she became part of "leadership." She promoted a supervisor to fill her former role. As usual, I was brought in to help mature the already talented Stephanie's leadership skills.

I was pretty harsh in our first conversation.

"Mark, I lead by example," she said. "I work harder than anyone, I know everyone's job better than they do, and they can count on me to pitch in at a moment's notice."

"So while you're busy doing your old job, who's leading the organization?"

Silence. (Clients find out quickly that I can sit in silence longer than they can stand.)

And then she took a deep breath, and said, "but they'll think I'm no longer part of the team, that I think I'm more important than them, that they can't count on me, that I just sit in my office and surf the internet."

Now we had something to work with. Quite a bit to unpack, in fact. But now the projections, beliefs, and insecurities were out in the open where we could sort through them.

Epilogue: In Stephanie's 360 review, (where I interview a number of people in the organization above and below the client) we got feedback that surprised her. The team thought she was the exact right person to promote. They loved working for her, and here's the kicker: they wished she would let go of more of the day-

Set Boundaries

Drown Out Critics

Commit to the Mission

to-day, trust them, and help grow the (
seat. She had made up all the criticism i

to-day, trust them, and help grow the organization from her new seat. She had made up all the criticism in her own mind.

By setting your boundaries, drowning out the critics, and committing to the mission:

You will get more done on what is important.

You will become more generous because you'll have more to give when it is needed.

You will be present, clear, and able to see what your people actually need.

You will be more cheerful and loving to be around.

You will be an incredible team player, because the team's mission will be a *10*, and you will be ruthlessly dedicated to weeding out distractions to said mission.

You will be, in reality, less selfish.

NEW LEADERS HAVE A HARD TIME REALIZING THAT SOMETIMES THEIR JOB IS TO JUST GO TO STARBUCKS AND THINK.

"Ohhhhh, I get it. You can't do *Only 10s* because …"

… only people like Richard Branson and Elon Musk are free to only do *10s*.

How do you think they became Richard Branson or Elon Musk? Many of the top performers in the world are maniacally focused. Relationships, well-being, and even kindness take a back seat to the pursuit of a goal. Watch any biography of Michael Jordon or Howard Stern and you will learn the cost of that pursuit. I'm not suggesting that kind of exclusion.

What I'm talking about is taking the gold and leaving the pathology. We are committed to a full life that includes relationships, self care, community, and impact. There are 100's of books that could satisfy the brain's need for certainty and that will tell you to stay up till 2 a.m. and then get up at 5 a.m., eat only raw meat, and stop only for CrossFit and tweeting about how amazing you are, to build that business. This isn't that book. Here, we want consciousness. Having a deliberate definition of success, and then making the choices to use our time and attention to build that life. One choice, one relationship, one action, at a time.

I don't want to be Jeff Bezos … I want to be the best, most fulfilled Mark Silverman I can be. That won't happen by default … I need to create him every day.

When I was transitioning my career from sales to coaching, I became very involved in my mentor Rich Litvin's community of 1000's of coaches. I was becoming known in those circles and my world revolved around those gratifying relationships. Half of my clients were other coaches, which was a good source of income, and I also contracted with Rich, for a sum of dependable money, to curate one of his programs. I loved the job and the people I got to talk to, and I believed in the program I was supporting. The income was essential for me to continue to support my family while growing my own coaching practice. The problem was, my own practice wasn't growing the way I wanted it to. It took a bit of introspection, but I finally saw why. Coaching coaches was not my calling. My heart and passion are in the glass buildings I pass by in every city. I love helping the men and women in business suits learn to thrive, open, and create impact and legacy. In fact, I live for that.

I remember being asked to teach sales techniques to Rich's group of coaches during an intensive workshop. I decided to wear my solid gold watch and the Hugo Boss suit I'd shelved for over three years. I had rejected that Mark for the softer more coachy Mark. Yet, putting on that persona after several years just felt right. It felt authentic. When I walked into the room, I got a different response from every person in the room. It was powerful. People even said, "Wow, this feels like the real you." I found it a bit shocking, if I'm being honest. That was when my good friend, Helen Appleby, a powerful executive coach said the phrase that changed everything, "Dah-ling," (she's British), "you belong in glass buildings."

I realized that supporting Rich, although I loved it, was a 9. I saw that I was a big fish in a pond I didn't even swim in. I needed the income. It felt like a solid *10* … but … it hid the real *10*. I needed to find my own inner Richard Branson and do what was right for me.

Terrified of this decision and the implications to my income, I called Rich and told him I could no longer do the work he contracted me for. He totally understood and it was the right shift of resources at the right time for his business as well. I didn't know where the replacement income would come from, but I was committed. I'd joined a couple of business clubs a month before and changed my focus to what was true for me. I found myself in the pond I wanted to swim in. To my surprise, the exact same day I finished my responsibility with Rich … I got the call to coach two young VPs who just got promoted, on the 19th floor of a beautiful glass building. And, it was for more money than I was making in the role I let go. Then another call a few weeks later from a seasoned, overwhelmed CEO came in. After that, a serial entrepreneur who wanted to go to the next level.

Now my practice is filled with *10s*. My people. I still take on a coaching apprentice each year, because I love sharing the journey and I believe in the impact of the profession. But most of my time is spent walking into glass buildings, coaching executives, and giving workshops.

Note: *Only 10s 2.0* was written in the time of COVID-19. Walking into glass buildings was not likely to be a realistic possibility in the near future. However, this shift and the magic of video conferencing kept me working with the people I made the biggest difference with. In fact, coaching during this crisis became one of the most fulfilling times in my career.

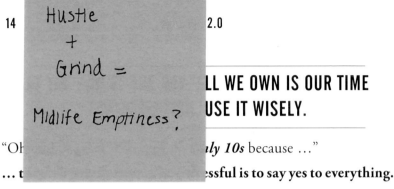

Hustle
+
Grind =
Midlife Emptiness?

LL WE OWN IS OUR TIME
USE IT WISELY.

"Oh … ly 10s because …"

… t …ssful is to say yes to everything.

"Successful people say yes to everything, really successful people say no to almost everything." Warren Buffett.

Most people think the hustle and grind cultures of Grant Cardone and Gary Vaynerchuk are the only ways to achieve success. The modern mind eats that crap up. And yes, hard work is the path to what we hope to achieve. But I think of "burning the candle at both ends" as pathology. It's fear based. And I don't want to live a life that is fear based. It is unsustainable. I have seen too much burn out to be fooled. I want to fill the teacup to overflowing and give from the saucer. Giving from an empty teacup leaves me drained, miserable and empty. Giving from the saucer is flow. It is abundance. It is joyful.

The only way to do this is by saying no to the things that keep us from accomplishing our goals, inhibiting our relationships, and limiting your self-care. You want the hustle and grind? This ain't that book. You want a rich, fulfilling, connected life, saying yes to ONLY those things that fit, being committed to true *10s*? Welcome home.

The hustle and grind culture is a lie. It is a sugar high for the ego. Like the corporate job it belittles, it also runs into the midlife emptiness brick wall. Hustle and grind can be beautiful things … but only in the context of a grounded consciousness.

What I learned in my years as a sales executive, and in teaching sales to individuals and teams, was that "qualifying" is one of the most impactful skills we can learn. In my sales career I was more of a big game hunter, preferring to create deep relationships and navigate multi-million- dollar deals that would take from six months to a year to close. My friends and colleagues, Kurt Greening and Seth being honest. That was when my good friend, Helen Appleby, a powerful executive coach said the phrase that changed everything, "Dah-ling," (she's British), "you belong in glass buildings."

I realized that supporting Rich, although I loved it, was a 9. I saw that I was a big fish in a pond I didn't even swim in. I needed the income. It felt like a solid *10* … but … it hid the real *10*. I needed to find my own inner Richard Branson and do what was right for me.

Terrified of this decision and the implications to my income, I called Rich and told him I could no longer do the work he contracted me for. He totally understood and it was the right shift of resources at the right time for his business as well. I didn't know where the replacement income would come from, but I was committed. I'd joined a couple of business clubs a month before and changed my focus to what was true for me. I found myself in the pond I wanted to swim in. To my surprise, the exact same day I finished my responsibility with Rich … I got the call to coach two young VPs who just got promoted, on the 19th floor of a beautiful glass building. And, it was for more money than I was making in the role I let go. Then another call a few weeks later from a seasoned, overwhelmed CEO came in. After that, a serial entrepreneur who wanted to go to the next level.

Now my practice is filled with *10s*. My people. I still take on a coaching apprentice each year, because I love sharing the journey and I believe in the impact of the profession. But most of my time is spent walking into glass buildings, coaching executives, and giving workshops.

Note: *Only 10s 2.0* was written in the time of COVID-19. Walking into glass buildings was not likely to be a realistic possibility in the near future. However, this shift and the magic of video conferencing kept me working with the people I made the biggest difference with. In fact, coaching during this crisis became one of the most fulfilling times in my career.

AT THE END OF THE DAY, ALL WE OWN IS OUR TIME AND ATTENTION, USE IT WISELY.

"Ohhhhh, I get it. You can't do *Only 10s* because …"

… the only way for you to be successful is to say yes to everything.

"Successful people say yes to everything, really successful people say no to almost everything." Warren Buffett.

Most people think the hustle and grind cultures of Grant Cardone and Gary Vaynerchuk are the only ways to achieve success. The modern mind eats that crap up. And yes, hard work is the path to what we hope to achieve. But I think of "burning the candle at both ends" as pathology. It's fear based. And I don't want to live a life that is fear based. It is unsustainable. I have seen too much burn out to be fooled. I want to fill the teacup to overflowing and give from the saucer. Giving from an empty teacup leaves me drained, miserable and empty. Giving from the saucer is flow. It is abundance. It is joyful.

The only way to do this is by saying no to the things that keep us from accomplishing our goals, inhibiting our relationships, and limiting your self-care. You want the hustle and grind? This ain't that book. You want a rich, fulfilling, connected life, saying yes to ONLY those things that fit, being committed to true *10s*? Welcome home.

The hustle and grind culture is a lie. It is a sugar high for the ego. Like the corporate job it belittles, it also runs into the midlife emptiness brick wall. Hustle and grind can be beautiful things … but only in the context of a grounded consciousness.

What I learned in my years as a sales executive, and in teaching sales to individuals and teams, was that "qualifying" is one of the most impactful skills we can learn. In my sales career I was more of a big game hunter, preferring to create deep relationships and navigate multi-million- dollar deals that would take from six months to a year to close. My friends and colleagues, Kurt Greening and Seth

Scharf had a different approach. They dealt in volume as "territory" managers. They were given all the small to medium opportunities. Five to ten of their deals equaled one of mine. And you know what, we were always together at the top of the leader board. My ADD and lack of organization made managing their volume of activity and opportunity management impossible. But they thrived and succeeded year in and year out where others struggled.

Their secret, beyond being knowledgeable, hard-working, and unstoppable? Discernment. I have rarely seen salespeople identify opportunities as viable or not, as quickly as Kurt and Seth did. They rarely wasted time. They perfected the criteria of a high probability sale (a **10**). But more importantly … and this was the key … they qualified OUT deals that were not going to happen. Less savvy salespeople would hold on to every deal, every possibility, ignore red flags, and spin their wheels. Others, with less skill, might waste precious resources (theirs and the company's) on things that were never going to happen. Did Kurt and Seth let go of some deals that might have closed? Absolutely. But the focus and streamlining of their chosen activities far exceeded the ones they took a pass on. We are all spinning our wheels on things that aren't going to pay off and they are sucking life and resources from the **10s** that will pay dividends for years.

I remember being asked to teach a workshop on large account management for our team. Seth walked in, rolled his eyes and said, "Silverman, what the %*&$ are YOU going to teach ME?" I said," Not a thing," and shrugged it off though I was a bit rattled, I'll admit now. After the workshop, he acknowledged that I did, in fact, teach him something. I said to him, "I could never do what you do, and you don't do what I do, and that works perfectly." Years later I am teaching and writing about what *he* taught *me* over a decade ago.

AT THE END OF THE DAY, ALL WE OWN IS OUR TIME AND ATTENTION, USE THEM WISELY.

"Ohhhhh, I get it. You can't do *Only 10s* because ..."
... you have too many responsibilities to only do *10s*.
Cart – Horse. Chicken – Egg. This is the really, Really, REALLY hard work that gets the train rolling. This is where many give up before they start. The story we tell ourselves is that the first difficult boundary, the first ask for help is out of reach because we are so over obligated.

So it feels like death to utter that first "No." Your internal chatter says, *I'd rather die than disappoint this person.* Just like day one of eliminating sugar from our diet, there is the withdrawal, and the cravings. It sucks with food, and it sucks with new behavior. That is why returning to victimhood feels so attractive. Just like a cookie relieves the craving, you want to say yes again to relieve the tension. But like any elimination diet, on day five or day six, you start to feel your brain clear, the weight drop off, and the joint pain subside ... setting a boundary, renegotiating agreements, and getting some damn help, starts to feel so ... freeing.

Mark, there is almost nothing on my to-do list. I feel free to create whatever I want.

I was hired to help Chris, the VP of Communications for a multinational organization raise his leadership game. Chris was the brilliant, incredibly competent, and hyper-responsible executive team member that a CEO could count on. Where others might drop the ball, Chris would saddle up his white horse (at 2 a.m. if needed) and save the day. He thrived on chaos, emergencies, and being able to fix the unfixable. It was his professional identity.

Where his professional life thrived however, his personal life wilted. Every romantic relationship possibility fell victim to his need to be "the responsible one at the organization." In my first meeting with Chris he made it clear that he didn't know any other way to operate and he only wanted me to give him tips on being "more productive." My job was to move him from "Superman Status," to a "Leader." I knew he would be more productive working with me … and I am a successful coach because I give people *what they need* **not** *what they think they want.*

The tell tale signs of the hero complex were easy to identify in his dialogue with me.

"Only I can do it correctly."

"I'm only going to have to re-do the work, after they do it."

"Nobody cares as much as I do."

"I wish everyone took this job as seriously as I do."

"I work until 2 a.m. every night."

"This place would fall apart without me."

On one level, Chris was right. He was the most competent member of the team. AND, he had trained everyone in the organization (his team members, the other VPs, and the CEO) that they could "give it to Chris," or do crappy work and "Chris will fix it." The CEO, overwhelmed herself, knew who to go to for help. She had asked me to help Chris find a "work-life balance," as well as develop as a leader, yet she also depended on his imbalance.

As a coach, this is a tricky needle to thread. What the CEO was asking, would impact her. I'll address that dynamic at the end of the story.

I had two cracks in the armor to work with. Chris was in a new relationship that seemed to have enough value to use as leverage for a shift. And, he was aware that the organization was an energy suck. Quickly, I was able to create a third crack in his opaque reality. He saw that he was *training everyone and everything to depend on him* and this was not the badge of honor he thought it was.   He now knew it to be a weight of his own making. Once seen, it cannot be unseen. I remember the turning point when he said, "Mark, I want a personal life." With that realization, the hard work began in earnest.

Did I mention Chris is incredibly talented? Well, he took to coaching with a new vengeance.

--He learned what belonged on his plate and what didn't. "Not my circus, not my monkeys," became his mantra when it came to other departments.

--He learned to discern which hills were worth "dying on," for the good of the organizations and began picking his fights more carefully.

--He learned to push unfinished or poor-quality work back to his team to improve, and to train, educate and support them to get better--always one of the toughest proactive skills a leader can cultivate.

--And … he learned to push back on his CEO, who needed this skill from her #2.

The result was that Chris' team became more and more competent, and although his "responsibilities" didn't change, his burden began lifting and his organization's productivity soared … and Chris took a long vacation with his new love interest (going on two years now).

Back to the CEO. Because the CEO was mature, and really did want the shift in her organization (she was being coached herself), she evolved with Chris. I taught Chris *how to push back* without causing chaos. He learned how to enroll the CEO and the other department leaders in the changes he was making.

WE TRAIN PEOPLE TO TREAT US EXACTLY HOW WE *NEED* TO BE TREATED.

"Ohhhhh, I get it. You can't do *Only 10s* because …"

… you don't know what you'll do with the blank page.

Scarier than setting a boundary or delegating a task, or even skydiving, is freedom. We all say we want it, and complain about not having it, but I call bullshit. When faced with space, choice, a blank canvas … most of us panic. Fill that shit up! My kids need me. The business is so demanding. I'm so needed. Anything other than experiencing the overwhelm that can come with free time and choice.

We are conditioned to react. We are built to create. But the noise and demands between those realities confuses us. There is a reason that freed long-term inmates commit crime to go back to jail. The big open world scares them now. We are no different.

The blank page can represent and confront us with so much inner questioning.

- Who am I without commitments and demands?
- Can I actually create from nothing?
- Where will I get my worth?
- People will judge my art (painting, writing, business) and my vulnerable expression.
- What if I'm wrong or bad or fail?
- Who am I to be free while everyone else suffers?

The pull back into overwhelm is strong. It is known. It is safe. It may be painful, but it is a familiar pain. Familiar is comfortable. The blank page is by definition unfamiliar, unknown and therefore very uncomfortable. Learn to be okay with uncomfortable, and the world is your blank canvas.

"Your job is to go to Starbucks and think." I need to make a challenge coin with this mantra embossed on it. Whether it is a CEO or a newly minted VP, their job is no longer "to do." It is to lead. Set direction. Be creative. Every successful leader I work with got there because they outworked, outperformed, and out cared everyone around them. But my job is to move them from the tactical, which is so satisfying to the ego, to the strategic, which is intangible. The tactical is filling in the boxes and taking the steps. The strategic is a blank white board that needs to be filled. It is the five- and ten-year plan. It is a new process, product, or division.

The muse (the creative force) comes to those who court her. That is true for music, writing, art … AND business. She needs space and avoids the turmoil of firefighting.

Remember the CEO I mentioned earlier who always had "ideas" that perished in the fires of overwhelm and busy? Once he delegated, created new leaders in his organization, and freed himself for a motorcycle ride, morning "jam sessions" with a pad and paper, and exercise (I really should buy stock in Peloton, since every client of mine now seems to own one) … he and the muse could flesh the ideas out. Bring the team in to explore possibility. Creating space is a game changer.

Remember, Warren Buffett said, "Successful people say yes to everything. Really successful people say no to almost everything." Yes, saying no creates laser focus, but it also allows for the blank page of creativity. Don't let the overwhelm of daily firefighting kill your ability to create from nothing.

WHAT WE PUT ON THE BLANK CANVAS IS AUTHENTIC, VULNERABLE, AND THEREFORE, UNCOMFORTABLE.

WHAT *ONLY 10s* TAUGHT ME

Practicing **Only 10s** required me to ask myself questions well beyond which task to focus on. It forcd me to ask the deeper questions.

Who am I?

What do I want?

What do I really want?

What gets in my way?

In the years that followed writing the original **Only 10s**, I answered these questions just as I encouraged my readers and workshop attendees to. I learned to take the actions, have the conversations, navigate the relationships, go too far, pull back too soon, give in to fear and breakthrough ... over and over again, sometimes treading the same path like we do in a video game to get to the next level. Fall down seven times, get up eight.

At times I feel discouraged by the self-help, self-esteem, spiritual enlightenment game and by extension I get uncomfortable with my part in it. I have grown in my own development and as a transformational coach. I know there are deeper, more profound shifts for humans to make in order to be "free." In part this is what caused me to be dismissive of **Only 10s**. (Remember how I was a hard No! at first?) I didn't want to be rearranging chairs on the Titanic by putting an updated edition of my book about "to-do lists" into the world. Then I dove into the writing and there, amidst the journaling to craft this introduction was the most important teaching of all for me.

Becoming conscious of my choices and why I made them as well as taking responsibility for creating my world with each decision ... were the first steps for me in the spiritual process. They are the beginning of understanding the power we all actually have in this life. *Only 10s* is a fundamentals course -- the fundamentals of choosing to-dos in this very moment.

The great masters agree, the path to true freedom is inquiry. Self-inquiry. The to-do list is relegated to low-level consciousness, and when evaluated, has us pausing to ask, "do I even want to do this?" We get to unpack each choice. We get to see what resentment has to teach us. This introspection awakens us to personal truths. *Only 10s* breaks the road to finding out *who we truly might be* into small doable segments. It paves the way to **Mastering Midlife** because we are looking at what we do, and how "what we choose to do" reflects who we truly are.

And I believe the secrets to the universe, your universe, which is the only universe (that counts, anyway) is in your to-do list. It's a bold statement, I know. There is so much to know about you based on what's on your list and why it's there. How you think and feel about your to-do list says a lot about you. You can go to a mountaintop ashram and meditate your way to freedom, or ... you could study, inquire, question, and interrogate the shit out of the what, why, and how you do everything you do (or don't do). The secret sauce is in the what, why, and how, which I call the "qualifiers".

Enlightenment, freedom, and truth are everywhere. Why not start in the immediate -- how we spend our time and where we place our attention.

The by-product of this practice, is a more pleasant, better run world for all who encounter you from their universe, and as satisfying and purpose filling as that can be, it's totally secondary.

Back to the reason for the work, any work ... we do all of this to improve our experience of our time on earth.

I do not know your purpose, and I do not know your mission. That is for you to create and decide. We could get into a spiritual debate on whether G-d cares or destiny has a hand in it, but that is for the next book. Right now I will use purpose and mission as compass points for how you spend your most precious commodities (and what we all have in common) -- our time and attention -- how we deal with linear time on this plane of existence ... human time on earth.

I have been to the mountain top. I've seen reality. I've been to heaven and hell. I've been one with the rocks on the desert, and explored the griefs of my childhood. I have been slave to cultish thinking and free of all human concerns. What I am left with today, and it may change in the next paragraph, is that *this is it*. This is the whole shebang ... this.

Your world. Your relationships. Your experiences. Your life, now as it is. There is no later and there is no other place to be. Yes, you are the universe, and it is comforting to know who you really are was never born and will never die ... it's freeing even. But who you really are doesn't pay the bills, chop your wood, or carry your water.

Which brings me back to your to-do list and how you spend your time. Clint Black, one of my favorite country singers named his albums for his perspective on life as he got older with "Killing Time" (1989), "No Time to Kill" (1993), Spend My time" (2004), and "On Purpose" (2015). Perspective changes, and I hope to change your perspective with this second edition of ***Only 10s***.

YOU HAVE NO TIME LEFT TO KILL, SO HOW YOU SPEND YOUR TIME NOW, IS HOW YOU LIVE THIS LIFE

So let's leave spiritual questions and truths on a shelf. It made me feel better to explore them and justify revisiting old territory. Let's also leave greater mission and purpose off to the side and pick it back up in a bit. My goal is to have you question the shit out of your day, to Marie Kondo (the touch everything person) the hell out of what's on your plate. I want you to recognize your victim, your honesty, as well as your lies to yourself, so you CAN create the life you want. Even if the life you have is overwhelming and demanding, you can *Only 10s* your life. You've been dealt a hand (you've chosen way more of the cards then it is comfortable to admit, perhaps), you can hold your ace, and trade in four of your five cards or you can discard and exchange, one at a time.

Courage, willingness, comfort, and circumstance will be your guide.

I'm a fold-the-entire-hand-and-reshuffle kind of guy. Rip off the bandaid and jump in. It's a bit of a roller coaster, and I don't recommend it, but it worked for me. Trust yourself to move at your own pace.

We will talk a lot about our own wants, needs, desires in this book. We will also talk about service, selflessness, and letting go of our own wants, needs, and desires. This is not a contradictory bug in the program, it's a feature. Wrestling with our humanity (wants, needs, desires) and our spirit (love, compassion, service) is where we start to master midlife. Humans have struggled with this for 1000s of years, since we started to reason, and imagine, and live in large groups. YOU will not figure it out in a week, or a month, or maybe ever. It is the figuring it out, getting in the arena as FDR and Brene Brown say, where the mastering happens.

I am going to ask a few things of you before you read on …

1. Keep an open mind. You can discard everything at any time after the experiment.
2. Dedicate yourself to uncovering uncomfortable truths.
3. Do not stretch the rubber band too far. Keep yourself safe until you acclimate.
4. Experiment. Play. Learn for yourself.
5. Love and forgive yourself and others as often as necessary. It's like vitamin C, it doesn't stick around, you can never have too much, and it's healthy as all heck.

Okay.

Ready?

Let's dive in.

INTRODUCTION

Maybe, like me, you've attended the seminars, bought the tools, practiced the principles and still failed "get organized," once and for all. If so, I'm sure you wondered, "How the hell can an intelligent, educated, successful person be so miserably inadequate at writing out a list of tasks and then accomplishing said tasks?" Perhaps we're kindred spirits.

I had a beautiful leather-bound Franklin Planner. I prioritized A, B, and C items. I forwarded my list from one day to the next. I worked on big rocks and let go of the small ones. For about two days.

I spent $1,500 and an entire day learning the "Getting Things Done" program. I loved that program and that system. I spent days listing everything, I bought a label maker to get my files organized and attractive. I touched nothing more than once. That lasted about a week.

Six months later, I took the refresher course, and reset. I got three days out of it that time.

The irony of my story is that I was a top salesman in the fast-paced and highly competitive IT world for 15 years. I won awards year after year, and earned millions for my employer. However, I felt constantly overwhelmed. I felt like a fraud because each situation was a last minute buzzer beater. I loved the adrenaline rush of being the hero that saved the quarter, but hated the stress and fear that came with never feeling in control. Distraction, procrastination and working on the wrong things had me feeling like a failure no matter how many times I exceeded my actual goals.

Unfortunately, I didn't know any other way. No matter what I did, I could not become organized, methodical, and deliberate. It was almost impossible to set a plan, follow the steps and execute. Except, at the last minute, when everything focused down, the deadline was looming and it was clear what needed to be done, I could block out all distractions, blow through any barrier, and close the sale.

Fear drove me every day. Fear of failure, fear of being found out. Adrenaline saved me at the last minute, over and over again. In my day to day, fog and confusion were my constant companions, which I learned later was undiagnosed ADD. Once diagnosed in my 40s, Adderall and Ritalin helped quite a bit, but only if I decided what to work on and sat myself down to do so. Otherwise, I could focus intently on researching the latest iPhone or a colleague's more pressing problem, forgetting about my own work, once again.

I didn't know it at the time, but there was a clue in that last minute buzzer beater ability to focus. Why am I great in a crisis? Why, when I decide I want a new car in the morning, can I have one in my driveway by that very evening? Why can my son (also diagnosed with ADD) sit down and figure out the new Verizon Fios menus and remote, but struggle with an English paper? Why does he know every baseball player, their stats, and where they are from yet he can't retain the information needed for a test in school?

"Mark, it's not true you can't focus. When you are excited by something, I've seen you focus and accomplish amazing things," my coach, Rich Litvin, said to me one day.

It's absolutely true that when I am interested in something, I can focus. When my son wants a goal, nothing will stop him. ADD stops being a factor. When it is a 10 on a scale of 1-10, something miraculous happens. It gets done. No tools, programs or seminars. It just gets done. Only every time.

So here you are.

You've picked up yet another book on "Time (please help me get organized) Management," or self-management, or getting things done – with the hope of some new method or insight that might flip a switch. Maybe this book will finally get you to hunker down and do what you know you should be doing.

This isn't that book!

What you have here are my notes and experiences of what happened after I realized that I actually do focus … when I give a shit. And I don't … when I don't.

I can share with you that once I let go and started trusting this "inner compass," amazing things happened. Time opened up, more and more got done, and I learned that I can trust myself to focus on what needs to be focused on most. I learned that this inner guidance of following what excites me, actually got my taxes done, insurance papers submitted, and an entire book written.

This discovery has worked a miracle in my life. I get stuff done. I get stuff done that is important to me. I can now trust myself to follow through on a large goal or vision because I have found my "why," and "want to," that is essential for me to actually care and focus.

As I discovered this new way of looking at the world, my life and business began to open up. I shared my insights with clients who also had big goals … and big distractions. As we went through their to-do lists, their eyes opened to the internal compass approach, and they too dropped the dead weight that made each day more difficult than it needed to be. They learned to trust themselves, and in turn found the energy to move forward on creative endeavors, creating whole new divisions and projects to move their businesses forward.

MY STORY
WHAT IT WAS LIKE

I'd review my agenda each morning, diligently and clear-eyed:

Big plans today! I know just who to call, and I have an idea for a marketing blitz. I really need to get the sales forecast done for my boss. It is due in three days, but if I start now, I can get all the info together. I have presentations at 10 a.m. and 2 p.m., and hopefully I can squeeze a haircut in afterward. I need to call my mom, and I want to check on my friend who had back surgery. Oh shoot, I need to get Jake to his baseball game by 5:30. Okay, I got it – if I just stay on track.

As the day went on, so did the internal dialogue:

So much to do today. I'm overwhelmed. How am I going to get it all done? If I were just more organized. If I were more disciplined. I'm capable of so much more. If I were firing on all cylinders, I'd be freaking rich! If they knew how much I didn't get done, I'd get fired! I know I met my goals this month, but what the heck am I going to do next month? I can't keep this up. I need a break. Why is everyone always asking me for stuff? Why can't I get any help?

I was exhausted before I started. Every day felt like a treadmill on full speed and if I stopped for a minute, I would fall off the back. Every day was full of anxiety. No matter how successful I was, and I was pretty successful, the feeling of being a fraud was a constant. The to-do list got longer and longer to the point that "work owed" was impossible to ever catch up. I payed attention to whatever had the most immediate consequence, and did that. Again, this flawed system that I had built seemed to work. It was just the constant feeling of doom that never left. And, everyone was living it, so this must be what success takes.

I had constant fantasies of getting sick, or fired, just to get some relief from the unrelenting barrage of demands. I hoped for anything to stop the madness. Resentment was a constant, because the world asked too damned much of me. "Yes, I'll pick that up." "Yes, I can get that to you." "No, I don't need help … I'm fine." You'd think my name was "Earnest." All things to all people all the time. I thought "Earnest" was a being a good guy, a stand up man … I didn't realize he was just being a martyr.

To add to the constant worry about being all things to all people, I wondered to myself, why I seemingly had to work three times as hard to get half as much done. Why did I feel lazy even though I never stopped? Why did I feel like I was using ten percent of my capacity? It was a relief to know there was a reason for my scattered path to every destination when I was diagnosed with ADD, but it still didn't change the impact on my well-being and self-esteem when it came to handling my ever growing to-do list. Ritalin was a fantastic tool. I could take it, and then if I could get myself to start a project, I could get two hours of good solid work done.

I was plagued by the thought, *Why can't I keep my word to myself?* I wanted to be the kind of person who said they would do something, then did it. Discipline. I needed discipline. If I just had more discipline I would be the kind of man I was supposed to be, I thought. The self-judgment and shame followed me everywhere.

WHAT HAPPENED?

One day, I was whining to my coach, "This ADD is kicking my ass! I have focused down to five projects that are really important to me, I take my Ritalin, clear the decks, and I still can't get my work done. It's driving me crazy!"

He was reassuring, and asked me to humor him, and we went through my projects one by one. For each one, we tested my commitment to the goals and needs of each project. In my coach Rich Litvin's language, life's opportunities were either a "Hell Yes" or a "Hell No." In my words, I described myself as a person with an On and an Off switch, though I fought it every step of the way. Together we used the scale of 1 to 10 to evaluate my task list.

They landed as follows.

Project 1. No question, I loved this one, it holds a ton of juice for me. This is a Hell Yes. A 10.

Project 2. This is my lifeblood. It is my business and the reason I do this work. Absolutely a 10.

Project 3. Very important to me, I want to do this. I love working with these people. I can't seem to get to it. I don't want to disappoint anyone though, I committed to it. Oh shit, this isn't a 10. It's more like a 9. No wonder I can't get to it.

Project 4. This one has to happen. I cannot delegate, the ball is rolling and the deadline coming. I will *not* let these people down. Boom, a 10.

Project 5. I get the game by now. No, this is a "should." I don't really want to do it but it seems crazy not to. A 5 at best.

I was left with three projects that, according to my internal compass, were filled with energy and motivation. Dropping the remaining two came with fear because I needed to have honest conversations about not really wanting to do them. I hated disappointing people I love and respect (and wanted to like me).

I had my *10s*.

And then I had my *Aha!* moment. I thought back to the years before I ran the Marine Corps Marathon.

My marriage had ended and my career was on the express elevator to the basement. I was having panic attacks, and got very sick, weakening my body and adding to my depression. As my health came back, and I got a new job, I wanted my kids to see how their dad handled adversity. I needed something crazy to snap me back. In hindsight, I needed a *10*. I recall listening to the radio, while waiting for another doctor appointment, when I heard Dr. Oz interviewing some "crazy" ultra marathon guy ... at least from my vantage point, ultramarathoning seemed a little crazy. He talked about green drinks, alkalizing, and how he believed that everyone could run, *everyone*. Bad knees, no muscle mass, bad back.

Can *I* run, I wondered? I grab on to the craziest things!

I got this guy's book, devoured it, and started the painful walk/ run of one mile per day.

Then two miles. Then three miles of slow jogging while filling my head with self-help books and audios of every flavor. A special shout out to Brian Johnson's *Philosopher's Notes*, for getting me through mile after mile. I made a decision. It was early March and against all good advice, I signed up for the 26.2 mile Marine Corps Marathon. I told everyone who would listen, and I raised thousands of dollars for charity, so there was no backing out. The impossible happened. I ran the Marine Corps Marathon with only eight months of running experience, let alone training, because it was a *10*.

My *10* looked like it was the marathon itself, but in actuality, it was deeper than that. The real, driving *10* was my kids – and the influence I had on them. The MCM was my task. And it was a difficult, resistance-filled task at that. An added *10* was in saving face. By raising all that money and being so public about my objective, I used my inner fear of looking bad to motivate me. Since *not looking bad* was a *10*, for me, sore knees became a 9.5.

How do I know the MCM was a *10* for me? Because I did it. And it was this clue that tipped my hand when Rich said to me, "Mark, nothing stops you when you really want to do something. ADD is not an issue, resistance isn't an issue, fear isn't even an issue. You just do it."

He was right. I couldn't believe it. Half the stuff on my to-do list had qualifiers. I *should* do this, I thought to myself. I was afraid of *not* doing this. What would people think if I said no? Once I addressed the qualifiers, I got clear on what I wanted to do and what I did not want to do. It was getting more difficult to lie to myself.

The conversation and realization exposed the self-imposed victim mentality I lived with. Nobody was making me do anything, I was *choosing* to do everything I did, and mainly because the choice of *not* doing it was something I wanted to avoid. Consequences had been dictating my *10s,* nobody was making me do anything. I would choose to *not* do something I really wanted to do because I wanted to avoid some pain or fear. I was always choosing. I let that sink in for a moment. I'm still letting it sink in.

I always do *10s.* My reasons for declaring something a *10* (or intuitively gravitating to it as such) just may not be apparent at first. More on this later.

WHAT IT'S LIKE NOW

I still have ADD. I still get easily distracted. I still rebel, resist, and I would much rather read a juicy news article than do my work.

What's changed? Everything!

By pausing for a moment and considering each task on my plate, or new request coming my way, I can consider my inner compass, and discern the motive for choosing whether or not I take it on. My thought process revolves around an internal flow chart with intersections consisting of various questions.

Do I want to or not?

Am I avoiding something unpleasant or is fear influencing my choice?

Is there a "should" anywhere in the equation?

If there is resistance, what is that about?

Do I have beliefs, real or imagined, that have undue influence over this decision?

Are they true?

Once I ferret out these qualifiers, everything changes. I feel freedom, I can think, and my perception of life slows down. I can hear my own inner voice of preference. I am clear about what I want to do and don't want to do.

The process of deciding what to do with my time has slowed down, so I can navigate all the inputs that go into making decisions, giving me the choice over responding to outside influences. Mostly, I am happy – for no reason – a lot more of the time.

More specifically, keeping the above in mind, I get more done. My to-do list gets done (completely!) almost every day. It is a much shorter, much more focused list, and it all gets done.

I end the day with energy and a sense of forward progress. If it goes on my list, I can trust myself to get it done. If I have resistance to a task, I have the energy and willingness to get past it. That, in and of itself, is a miracle.

The only discipline I really need is to <u>slow down and pay attention so I can make a choice.</u> For the first time in my life, I feel like I have moved from Potential to Action.

WHAT IS A *10*?
(AND WHY SHOULD YOU CARE?)

A **10** is a "Hell Yes". It is an *all in, nothing's gonna stop me, I want this more than anything* feeling. You will know it is a **10** because you're doing it now, or you're clear that nothing and no one can stop you from doing it. Think about that *one thing* you did that seemed crazy or impossible and you did it anyway.

When you finally lost the weight …

When the client said no three times and you closed the sale anyway …

When you broke up with that wrong partner, for once and for all …

When work demanded you show up, and you were at your kids championship game anyway …

What were you thinking? What was your mindset? How did you handle obstacles? What was different in each case?

There are really very few "true **10s**". But once you look, really look, they become clearer and easier to spot. Once you experience how a **10** looks, tastes, and feels, it ruins your 7s, 8s, and 9s forever. The Marine Corps Marathon shattered my illusion and showed me exactly who I was, and what I was capable of, *when I am committed to doing something.* A **10**!

We can categorize **10s** in several ways.

While each of the attributes support each other, it is not essential to build an interlocking complicated system. If it was, I couldn't sustain it. I need simple.

The three categories worth our attention are **Big Picture *10s***, more immediate or **This Week's *10s*** and – front and center – **today's *10s***.

Let's start with what is most important. Today. Right now.

What is a *10* for Today?

Today's 10s
You really want to do it.
Deadline, due date, or
consequence if not done today.
Anything Scheduled.

Below is an actual conversation with a client about the pressing items on his list. It is early in the week, he is already overwhelmed, has competing commitments, and a mixture of personal and professional responsibilities. Sound familiar?

Today's List
8am Mark
9:30am Vendor Meeting
11AM VP meeting
Two offer letters
2pm Interview
Book CA trip
Backfill Network Admin
Assisted living for my mom
Email
Presentation for all hands
I want to get to the gym
Back to school night for kid

First, we go through the appointments scheduled. Do they need to happen? Does he need to be present or can he send a proxy? Then we move on to the tasks crowding the plate. We question each item on the list and, one by one, make them prove they need to be on the list for today.

IF IT IS GOING TO BE ON THE LIST, IT NEEDS TO FIGHT TO GET THERE.

In the example, the two offer letters are for quality candidates waiting to come aboard and fill open positions that, left empty, are burying him and his team. They absolutely stay. The California trip isn't for three weeks, so it is not a *10* for today and it can wait. He still may book his trip today, but it takes no room on the now exclusive and preciously protected *10s* list. Backfilling the Network Admin is a project (meaning, there are multiple steps/actions to be taken) – and the only active action item is to send a job description to personnel. That 5-minute action replaces the more time consuming (and overwhelming) project as a whole. He desperately needs that position filled, so taking action toward that happening is a *10* for today. He now realizes he could ask his brother to gather four websites for places for their mom, so we decide this is now another project and just a single action item gets the *10* for today. "Assisted Living for Mom" project is reduced to a quick email making the ask of his brother. The all-hands meeting is tomorrow, and that presentation needs to be done today (but only if he wants to be prepared). He doesn't have to do it, he could wing it (victim), but he wants to crush it, so he chooses to spend the time (empowered). The presentation itself is not a *10*, it is the *outcome* of an outstanding presentation that provides the energy to pull him through the task. Seeing himself successful on stage creates an excitement and a want for the project. He missed his window for going to the gym. It will not happen in the afternoon today (if we tell the truth about it), and consequently it comes off the list.

We try never to lie to ourself about anything on our list. If the gym is really a *10*, he will be there tomorrow morning. Email is never a *10*. It fills in the gaps and is a low-yield activity. A response to a specific email can be a *10*, but mindlessly clearing your inbox must be treated like Facebook and the news. And, I do have clients who time-block (more on that later) an hour for their email per day as a *10*.

A Real *10* <u>needs</u> to get done,
<u>needs</u> to get done <u>by me</u>,
and <u>needs</u> to get done <u>by me, toda</u>y.

(or I just want to and it doesn't interfere with a consequential 10).

The new list of **Today's *10s*** for this client looks like this:

<u>Today's List</u>
☑ 8am Mark
   9:30am Vendor Meeting
   11AM VP meeting
   Two offer letters
   2pm Interview
   Job description to HR
   Ask Fred to search 4 places
   for mom.
   Presentation for all hands
   Back to school night for kid

What changed in his day? Look at the new list. The meetings were deemed important. The meeting with me is done, so it gets a check. The premeditated failure of not going to the gym is eliminated, and no longer takes up space on the list, nor in his head. Two in-depth items are now reduced to the five-minute tasks and are part of moving major projects forward (Description to HR and Note to Brother), so a couple of heavy projects no longer crowd today's list and overwhelm him. He now knows that even email takes a back seat to the presentation tomorrow. He may have gotten lost in his inbox and at 11 p.m. he'd find himself working through the night. He now has plenty of space to make an impact on stage the next day. His kid is a *10*, so he will be at the school, calm and present, and with the confidence that he did the *right* things today.

Can you feel some breathing room? A little less tension? He certainly did, and said so.

Yeah, but.

But what about interruptions? The email needs to get done, people expect answers. Yes, they do. This is where the work comes in. This is where I learned the most about myself, and my ability to prioritize my day. If I got into a car accident, I would not be available for last minute interruptions and I wouldn't be on email. The decision would be made *for* me because something unavoidable came up. That would miraculously prioritize my life.

Giving in to (most) interruptions is disrespectful to 10s.

It's tough, but action item number one needs to be to stop the bleeding. Our *10s* need to have that level of urgency, respect, and commitment. The time and focus will not miraculously appear. We must find it, and fight for it, in order to make sure it gets done, *because we decided it was the right, most important thing to get done.*

If the two offer letters and the presentation are truly *10s*, if they will make the biggest impact in my client's life, then they are as important as a car accident. If he could blow off the presentation and wing it on stage, or let the offer letters slide, then they were not a *10* to begin with – and did not belong on the list for that reason.

A *10* is the "if I only got this one thing done today, it would be a great day," kind of thing.

I repeat, if you can let it slide, plan to *maybe* let it slide, or you won't fight for it, it is not a true **10** and does not belong on your list. It's time for you to learn to be honest with yourself. You can still do anything you want to do, put anything you want on your list, but be honest. If you don't do it, you've learned that other things truly do take precedence. And tomorrow you have a little more awareness when making your choices. This thing works whether you do it right or not … it is about awareness, choice, and responsibility for your actions.

This is a simple program. It ain't easy, but it is simple. Sometimes the **10s** list is one thing. Just one. I tell my clients that they can be interrupted all day, do email, read Facebook, go play with their kid, the world is their playground – but if there is an item on the to-do list that *is* truly a **10**, get that one item completed and watch it change everything. Then don't worry about the rest of the day.

> *Warning: **10s** are addictive. Once you find out you can defend your time, and feel the freedom, you will go back for more. Time sucks become irritating.*

As with everything worthwhile, this is a practice. I learned more about myself by setting a boundary and saying no than in many week-long workshops.

I once created an episode of the Mastering Midlife podcast called "Show me your to-do list and I'll tell you what you value."

I can learn a great deal about the deep inner workings of any client, just by going through their to-do list. Stay with this experiment and within three days you will start to see a shift. Even if you quit, nothing will be the same after. They say an AA meeting will ruin your drinking (and you may drink for ten more years.)

A few days of **Only 10s** will ruin your enjoyment of overwhelm forever.

Now, let's go bigger.

How do I know what I want to do each day? I mostly follow my excitement and energy, trusting that the flow will lead to more goodness than my past fighting and struggling ever did. I didn't come to this easily. It took months of trial and error, learning where I lie to myself and where I can trust myself. So although I follow this intuitive path, I do give it direction by using a compass. I ground myself in a well-vetted list of projects, my *Big Picture **10s*** that are deeply meaningful to me. The desire, excitement, and commitment to work on these stated projects *(**10s**)* overcomes my desire for shorter-term "cool stuff" that inevitably vies for my attention. I do get off track, but the program miraculously resets every morning, when I honestly ask, what is my **10** for today?

Shiny objects lose their luster
when the pot of gold shines just as bright …

Or, distractions lose their power when I am passionate about and committed to a really juicy project.

Warren Buffett speaks about a conversation he had with one of his staff. Buffett asked him to write down 25 things that he really wanted to accomplish this year. After the list was done, Buffett asked him to identify the top five that he really wanted to focus on. The man presented the list and Buffett asked, "When will you work on the other 20?" The man answered, "Whenever I can find the time and I am not working on the five."

"NO!" said Buffett, "You avoid those other 20 like poison."

Focus … and vehement boundaries!

I had five items on my list when I had my conversation with my coach, Rich. Turns out two of those items were not **10s** and so they did not belong in the top five. Dropping those two freed me up to focus even more, because I recovered the energy and focus from the work I was doing toward them. That focus and energy were compounded further because I let go of the fear, anxiety, and guilt I had associated with spinning my wheels on those projects.

Mark Zuckerberg of Facebook is famous (now infamous) for being maniacally focused on his company's solitary goal: Grow Facebook. Every idea, every project his team brought to the table, he would ask, "Does it help us grow?" If it didn't fit into that one area of focus, it was taken off the table

That got me thinking. If the smartest and most successful people drive towards one goal, what is mine? If I use my language, what is my ultimate *10*? Do I even have a single *10*?

I did some research. I thought about recent conversations with my clients, and found some interesting observations. Some had a clear goal or vision already. They knew what they wanted to build, so we were able to work backwards from that end goal to determine which projects would be *10s* in that context. Then we would build a plan, gather resources and march. Pretty straight forward.

Others did not have an ultimate goal and were searching. These were my "explorers." They were the already successful clients who have finally allowed themselves to think outside the box of their existing busy lives and careers, and look at more possibilities. The choice in direction were endless. How were we going to narrow down the paths to a truly satisfying and exciting next chapter?

With these clients, we focused on values, current projects, and personal inventories to start to form that "one place" on the map to strive for. Often it was a direction without a destination, but it was a clear direction.

I call it the **compass**.

True north is necessary to identify, and keeps us from straying too far off the path. I fell in love with this process of clarifying life's direction, and I saw it add rocket fuel to my client's lives, so I will dedicate a chapter to helping you find your own true north later in this book (Finding True North).

But for now, let's stick to helping you win the day.

FALSE *10s*

Earnestness

Netflix False Beliefs Shiny Objects

Fear Facebook

Addictions Should Boundaries 9.9s

News Juicy

Looking Good Other People's 10s

Because I can

The "Attention Economy" is out to get you.

So many things feel like a **10**, but absolutely aren't. Some are obvious, like social media and the news.

They suck me in, with their juicy and enticing headlines. Marketers (and friends) know everything I want from a **10**: a quick hit, a distraction, an emotional response, anything to get that dopamine going instead of dealing with the task in front of me. You actually don't stand a chance. There are 100,000 engineers, designers, and psychologists being paid billions by companies vying for your attention. The research that goes into you and I responding to our phone alerts like lab rats would astonish you. These obvious distractions are clearly not **10s**, but they are still addictive. I'm sure you know the inventory of your own false **10s** all too well. They acted like a *10*, because they get your interest, and they imply priority by holding up a sign like Wile E. Coyote to the Roadrunner, that reads, "I'm a *10*," look over here. Again, marketers, headline writers, and a whole lot of people know how to write enticing headlines and pitches to get us to believe the choice to engage with their content, product or service is our next *10*.

**False *10s* steal the only things I really own --
my time and attention.**

Addictions are False *10*s that can sometimes drive our lives. The relief from an uncomfortable feeling, or a difficult task, is a *10* if we slow down enough to notice. We are designed to look for quick hits of comfort and relieve pain. This can come from something as benign as a cookie here and there, or lead to the devastation of alcoholism. I lump the seemingly harmless and the life-threatening together to illustrate a point, but I do not take either of them lightly.

Addictions do not fight fair, and I have no illusion that this program will alleviate what has baffled man for centuries. If addiction is kicking your ass, I strongly encourage you to seek help. I know that territory and the life beyond it. As of now, ~~25~~ make that 30 years sober, I implore you to do so.

That said, finding recovery after hitting a bottom from an addiction is when living becomes the *10*, even as the addiction unfairly fights, dirty tactics and all as a 9.9. Life-threatening addiction aside, the equation still applies. Whatever we use for respite from our feelings, fears, and pain becomes a *10*, and once habituated, keeps us from even the most honest of pursuits. In Alcoholics Anonymous they say "think the drink through," meaning anticipate the consequences to the end. Though recovery involves quite a bit more than intellectual curiosity, the exercise can often unlock the hold the addiction has on us, if we simply and firstly interrupt the impulse. I have joked that political Twitter is my crack. I would much rather have a passionate argument, feel the

> What is my role, as the boss, of other peoples' 10s?

outrage, and be "right" than focus o[n] ⋯
necessities like paying my bills and ⋯s
a trap. It's a distraction, and I do n[e] ⋯
my *10*s … from my own life.

outrage, and be "right" than focus on monotonous and low-passion necessities like paying my bills and following up on emails. But it's a trap. It's a distraction, and I do not want it taking me away from my *10*s … from my own life.

**Other people's *10s* are not my *10s*,
unless I choose them to be, and then they *are* mine.**

When we make other people's priorities our own they are *False 10s.* When we consider choosing them to be a *10* for us, we have to admit to ourselves that what we are really wanting is to please someone else by making this choice. Of course, it can be a *10* if we want to support someone, but I am talking about the times when we do it for other than altruistic reasons. Pleasing, being a good guy, invoking our alter ego, I named mine "Earnest," or simply not dealing with the annoyance of the asker is actually the *10*, not the task itself.

If you have ever had a coworker adept at the "cold bristle manipulation," perhaps you know what I mean. "Oh, I'll just take care of it instead of dealing with Herb's wrath," means that avoiding Herb's tantrum is the *10*, while doing what you wanted to do is the 9.

Get it? We are ALWAYS choosing.

Now here the converse can be true. Someone can ask you to do something *you really don't want to do*, but the person asking is a *10* for you. Investing in that relationship is a *10*. Now you can consciously and cheerfully pick up the task as your *10*, because now it is.

I was coaching a client who had committed to helping at a charity event one evening. He was grumpy and angry with himself for saying yes. He was well trained in *10*s and saw his mistake, which made him even grumpier. He wanted to pull a no-show because it was a "should".

I talked him through this.

"Is it a cause you believe in?" I asked. "Yes."

"Are they people you value?" Again he said, "Yes."

"Did you commit, and will changing your mind have an impact?" He signed, "Ugh … Yes."

"Then your job is to choose to show up, stop being a victim, and cheerfully be of service," I said.

He later reported that he had a blast, the event was a huge success and that my voice was in his head all night, "choose to show up and cheerfully serve." It changed his whole mood.

If I catch myself thinking "I *should* do this," I stop.

I have a few alarms that go off in my head. When I hear myself say "I should do this," I immediately stop.

I ask more questions.

"Why *should* I do this?"

"Do I *want* to do this?"

I hold it up to the *10s* criteria:

Does it need to be done?

Does it need to be done now and by me?

Do I want to do it?

I pause. I evaluate. And I choose.

It only gets to be a *10* if it passes the internal interrogation. It is society's job to tell you what to do, who to be what is right, what is appropriate, and to be irritated when you don't comply … it is YOUR job to choose to comply or not.

MEET EARNEST

Earnest is my alter ego.

The conditioned carrier of my False *10s*. He is the nicer, harder working, "always there for people" other self. It's not that I am not a kind or helpful person, it's just that Earnest, in his earnestness, often makes me look and feel bad. Earnest will say "yes" to every project, every committee. Earnest will stop at the store dog-tired, take on the extra work, stay late so you can go home, and apologize for not doing enough. Earnest will hide being tired and stretched too thin, his resentments, and even his opinions, if they will cause others to be uncomfortable.

Earnest is more pretzel than man.

Earnest is too polite, too useful, and a joy to everyone who meets him. Remember in the introduction, my ex-wife said "everyone likes Mark." They liked Earnest, not Mark. Nobody even knew Mark.

Earnest is a nightmare for *10s*. He will give them up in a heart beat. Earnest is the nicest, most benign, yet deadliest enemy you will ever meet. He will give away your precious time and attention, and stop you from asking for help. He will kill your focus, your energy, your progress, and maybe even compromise your health. Beware of Earnest.

Exercise from the *Only 10s* Workshop:

Who is your Earnest? Name him or her.

How do they show up? Be detailed.

What do they cost you?

Now you will see them show up at every turn … you will hate them at first … but you will learn to laugh at them and drain them of their power. They are nothing but a conditioned self, that over time will weaken.

Fear underlies most False *10s*

I am amazed at the amount of time and life that fear has stolen from me.

Fear is my other alarm bell. It used to be that I would skip over the fear and go right to the task (or avoid the task) without noticing that sneaky motivation. I didn't notice my life getting smaller and smaller because of all my little daily fears. Now I can slow it all down enough – my racing thoughts and my overwhelming feelings – to feel the fear, understand its roots, and decide.

Fear isn't always overt ... often it is hidden under our choices, and can only be seen if we slow way down, and feel.

Over time, fear gets easier to spot. Once I slow down enough to see and feel the fear driving a choice, I can lean into what I fear. The fear of disappointing someone, fear of looking bad if I say no, fear of being left out, or fear of other people's beliefs, all buffet me about whether consciously or unconsciously. I say I don't want to dance and maybe even think it's true ... but really, I want to get up to dance, I'm just afraid to be the first one up there.

When avoiding fear is the *10*, I lose.

I drew a line in the sand when I recognized the cost of giving into fear. I no longer wanted fear to steal my precious time and attention.

False *10s* are sneaky.

False *10s* offer a wonderful cocktail of outsized promise (relief of some sort), and a chase that helps focus us in on something safe (relief from boredom, stress, confusion, or a difficult choice). There is something wonderful and comforting about losing myself in something – *anything* – even if it is not what I really wanted to be doing. Every day, every minute, offers me too many choices and I get overwhelmed. For me, everything comes at the same volume (ADD), which makes turning to the news for a dose of injustice a welcome distraction. Outrage is a wonderful way to focus, thus my political Twitter habit.

I have begun the practice of looking at False *10s* as if they are any deadly addiction. I think through the drink, when I remember. The moment I can pause and get conscious of what I am chasing,

I am at the point of choice. It takes practice, practice, practice, but eventually, when the bell of a False *10* rings, we don't have to answer it.

Believe me, I have shopped for and bought new cars just to have a compelling project rather than face the mundane of everyday life. If I can spot a False *10*, so can you. I've had the same car for over three years now. Given that one of my favorite False *10* habits is shopping for new cars, I would say something must be working.

I am not a victim of the world's priorities and interruptions.

Every day is a minefield of False *10s*. There are choices and prioritizing is essential. We are asked to lead the PTA, our kid gets sick, a fun opportunity comes along, or a compelling "emergency" crops up at work. It can feel like an endless barrage of "my life is not my own," and "I have no choices." But it's not true. It takes work and practice, and over time, things can shift. When we change how we view our world, our world shifts.

I go through this process with everything that comes into my world. What started as a painful and deliberate exercise while I was learning, has become a simple, 30-second contemplation. Sometimes I am presented with a difficult choice or dilemma, and I still need to write it out or talk with someone. Writing it out, or phoning a friend, helps me figure out if something I want to do, that feels suspect in its *10*-ness, will really bring me the outcome I think I am seeking. Journaling, a posse you can trust, and quiet time are all great ways to uncover False *10s*.

Putting it all to the test

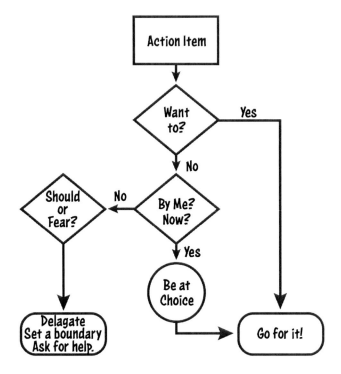

Let's take an everyday interruption that can derail a well-planned day. Your child has a sore throat. They really *should* go to the doctor and get a strep test. We have ourselves a very compelling, "should." We get that crushing, overwhelmed feeling (and feel like a bad parent for feeling it).

Clearly, I do not want to do it. I'm busy! I have a meeting, a project due, an unsympathetic boss. But it needs to be done (now), and I am the only one around.

Am I a victim? It certainly feels that way.

Once I get the initial grumble of annoyance out, or deal with the fear of what this means for my day, I can pause and take back my life. (Always easier said than done). This may seem like a small distinction, but this simple exercise can change my whole day, my mood and how I treat my sick kid. Bigger choices will come down the pike with the same dynamic, making this good practice. Practice, Practice, Practice.

So, how do I move from a victim of circumstance to the owner of my time and attention? Find the *10* and choose. I am a father. I love my kid. I want my kid healthy. I want to care for my kid. I know these are *10s*. I will take him to the doctor, because caring for my kid is a *10*. And, of course it is. But that extra 30 seconds changes everything. The shift is not unlike my client in the previous section who needed to show up for the charity event. Shifting from "I don't want to do this but will, to I want to take care of my kid, is the secret sauce of empowerment. If I can catch myself, and my woe is me attitude, and flip it to an empowering choice, it becomes habit. That habit slowly changes the way I see and relate to my world. I learn and experience that I am always at choice. I have always been at choice. I really can choose not to take the kid to the doctor, or I can choose to wait until tomorrow. There is a consequence to that. My kid could get sicker, or I will deal with the thoughts that I did not care for our kid in the way I believed necessary. They are unpleasant choices, but they ARE choices. Moving from "I have to" to "I chose to" is the secret.

It takes work to eat a salad instead of a piece of pizza, but over time, it changes everything.

False *10s* are our enemies. Find them. Be ruthless. Guard the only resources you ever truly own: your time and your attention. Yes, it takes work, practice, resolve, and commitment to live your *10s* ... and your life. And it IS your life.

I don't want to do it, but it needs to be done!

In his amazing book, *Relax Into Wealth*, Alan Cohen has a chapter titled, "If it's not fun, hire it done." What a freeing revelation. There are so many tasks I hate to do, that I am not very good at, or I do not have real time to do. Often, someone else can breeze through them in an hour where it would take me four, not counting the time to get ready to take on the task, walk around the task, and finally force my way through the task.

As a salesman, I racked up a large amount of expenses each week while entertaining clients, traveling, etc. The money came directly out of my wallet until I submitted the request for reimbursement, and the company paid. The charges averaged $2,000 per month of real, cash money. Most of my employers had rules (some would bend, some would not) of getting the expense report submitted within 60 days or I wouldn't get reimbursed.

When I submitted six months of expenses twice a year (often over $10,000 each), I would get some serious and understandable blow-back, because that was undermining the operational integrity of the finance group. The admonishment from management was small (a 9) compared to the agony (the *10*) of finding receipts, remembering appointments, mileage or meals well after the fact, and wondering how much money I had ultimately lost just because I couldn't find or remember an expense long after it was incurred.

My admin offered her help. "Mark, send me your receipts and mileage each week, and I'll submit your expenses for 10%."

I had a choice. Averaging $20,000 a year of expenses at 10% is $2,000. That is a lot of money. What good business person would give up $2,000 per year? I should get organized and do it myself, right? But wait, let's do a pragmatic cost analysis of this offer. Reporting some six months of expenses took me approximately six to eight hours each time. I made an average of about $500 per hour when I was working on revenue-producing work. That meant just the act of creating expense reports was costing me $500 X 6 = $3,000 in opportunity cost. I also dropped out at least 10%, if not more, of my expenses, due to inattention and disorganization, another $2,000.

My admin, in contrast, was a master of spreadsheets, so it took her a quarter of the time to complete the task. Add to it that she loved the extra "found" spending money from taking on a little side job. In turn, she loved me, too! Never underestimate the value of a loyal admin to a disorganized salesman. Remember, I had agonized over every element of the process, made mistakes, dropped receipts, and got grief constantly while I attempted to do this for myself. Plus, it was on my to-do list every week, causing me guilt and stress whether I did the task – or worse, let it go.

Human nature (or at least, my nature) will minimize the pain at first when confronting the dollar amount to be paid out to delegate, or admit we need help. I will discount the opportunity cost, because I can always do it on the weekend, or over two evenings. If you can do it, will do it, and the savings is worth it – go for it.

But if your reality resembles mine (Earnest doesn't always do what he *thinks* he will do), stop lying to yourself. I did and I took my admin up on her offer. It was more than worth it to me. In hindsight, and the more I do *this* work, I see even more benefits to "hiring it out."

And I have ever since.

This entire book is a game plan to beat back Earnest, stop pushing every boulder uphill, and find some breathing room. When I get breathing room, I get creative, and make better choices that improve every area of my life.

So I hire it out. I let go of what I am not good at, which gives me time to do what I *am* good at. I get more bang for my buck (or my time). I let go of that familiar vice grip of "should, have to, and dread," leaving me room to have a productive creative thoughts instead.

With the skill of hiring out, I create opportunity and relationships with other people whose strengths complement mine. And I don't have to submit my #*(% expenses, *ever*!

But shit has to get done, whether I want to do it or not!

I hear you. I hear it in my own head. Yes, shit needs to get done. But when the mind is barking its orders, the question to ask is "Which shit?", "Does it really?" "By whom, and by when?"

This inquiry goes a long way to quieting the barking.

I went against my own advice recently. I painted my office to save the money. Earnest thought it would be easy. It took me three days, and I did a pretty good job. My handyman painted my entire basement in one day, and it is perfect. I'm never painting a room again. In fact, my handyman can build a wall unit, fix a ceiling fan, and replace a toilet. Only I can write my book, coach my clients, and enjoy my kid's baseball game.

Hire it out.

Delegate.

Take the consequences consciously.

Or make it a *10*.

You are NEVER a victim. You always have choice.

FEAR

Fear is such a huge factor in my day-to-day actions that it deserves its own chapter. Fear causes global chaos, war, political vitriol, divorce, and all sorts of nastiness in the world. Fear sucks!

Everyone wants to dance.
Even the wallflowers want to dance, they are just afraid.

I have no idea who's expression this is (above), but when I read it, I was busted. My ex-wife loved to dance, and would be the first one on the dance floor, no matter the situation. When I drank, I danced all the time. Sober, I only danced when eight or more people preceded me. I would say I didn't want to dance, but that was the lie (I even told myself). I wanted to dance, it looked like fun, but I couldn't step out.

Until (counting people)…6…7…8…now I can dance. Pppphhheewww!

I want to dance, sing, and draw. I want to play softball, stand on stage, write, make videos. To say I don't is bullshit. It's hiding behind fear. Admitting that I want to do so many things is the first step. Dealing with the fear, and getting past it is the growth and the work.

People asked me to speak about wealth creation on after I became successful. I'm not sure my answer was what they expected.

"Mark, would you share how you made so much money? How could we be like you?" they'd ask.

"That's easy. I'm terrified every day. I have no self-esteem. I'm not cool. One day I realized I am never not going to be terrified, I will probably never have self-esteem, and no matter how hard I try, I will never be cool. I get up every morning when I don't want to, and show up, and do it all anyway. That's it. That was my secret weapon," was my reply.

When I got my first sales job at a high tech start up, I woke up with dread every day. The hiring manager did his best to warn me about the pace, the pressure and the impossible expectations. I talked my way into that job before my brain could talk me out of it. I would steel myself for a day of being so far out of my comfort zone that I couldn't see dry land. In hindsight, my *10* was an opportunity to provide for my family, and the fear was a 9.9. One day, I had a realization that reframed that fear and changed my beliefs about being fearful. I remembered being a waiter at the Four Seasons hotel. I remembered how I felt at the beginning of every shift, as the rich and famous, world leaders, and self-important people would be sitting in my section expecting impeccable service. I was terrified. I would literally sweat while I was polishing the silverware. I realized that I was always terrified – as a waiter, a student, on a date. It didn't matter the scope or the engagement, the fear was the same. This high-end, intimidating job was no different. If I was terrified as a *waiter*, I might as well be terrified and make a ton of money.

When something is a *10*, fear is not an issue.

A 9.9, and fear wins! Fear loves to play *10*.

True *10s* bump fear out of top billing.

Fear will look like resistance.

Fear will look like confusion.

For me, it is the root of all indecision, of over analyzing, and it is behind the exhausting choices that feel like rolling a boulder uphill. It will get me to say and believe things that are not true to avoid what I *really* want to do. When fear is a **10** and my want is a 9.9 or below, fear wins. It's that simple.

Conversely, when I want something so badly that I blow past fear, I know it is a **10**. I would fight a bear to protect my kids. There is a clue here. Terror is one thing, but when fears are small and quiet, they are insidious and can place a fog between me and what would probably be a **10**. That's where contemplation, inquiry, and discernment come in.

Fear of making the wrong choice. Fear of what people will think. Fear of losing out.

As I went through this process, and saw just how much these little fears dictated my choices and actions, I started to get angry. *Am i not going to dance because of what the people sitting at the tables will think? Really? That's the equation I live by? Really?*

When I slowed down and saw the fear for what it was, I was once again at choice. I still gave into fears daily, in small and large ways. But now I can see what it cost me. I now find it unacceptable for fear to keep me from using my time and attention for what I want in life. So I practice leaning in. I choose where to risk and experiment. Every time I chose to go past the fear and act, or speak, or say no, that muscle gets stronger. And my life gets bigger.

WEEKLY AND DAILY PRACTICES

Through practice and awareness, I earned my freedom and started the train of productivity rolling. Through trial and error, I found my white board, my journal and my calendar to be the three tools I need to keep focused on my *10s*. I am no longer a fan of having a ton of lists to keep track of and keep updated. Instead, I have learned to trust that if something wants to be important, it will make itself known, eventually. So I created this very simple system where I keep track of my *10s* on three small and focused lists.

Radar	This Week's 10s	Today's 10s
Action Items that will become a 10, but are not now.	Absolutely must be or wants to be done this week.	You really want to do it.
Deadline or due date (should be put on calendar when date known)	Once scheduled put on calendar	Deadline, due date or consequences if not done today.
		Anything scheduled

Radar

I use the Radar List for things that I know are important, are not a *10* this week, yet I don't want to lose sight of. The only criteria for inclusion on this list: I know these items will be a *10* at some point. Many things can be scheduled, and if you are good with your calendar for non-meeting type prompts, I wholeheartedly support you using it. But for me, there are some things I am not ready to commit to, so I cannot schedule those yet. I have done it before and just blown them off. Remember, the goal of self honesty? They are still important enough to become a *10*, so I want to keep track of them until my attention makes them so, or a compelling event forces them onto a list.

Watch your Radar. It is not a catchall for all the things you don't want to forget. Keep it short.

The dentist is the perfect Radar item for me. I know I need to go, but I do not like to commit to an appointment six months in advance. If I put it on my calendar to schedule, I will push it – week after week. So it goes on my Radar List the first week it comes to my attention. I'd love to be the kind of person who schedules it the moment the alert comes up, but I am not. It has to be a *10*, or I don't do it. Essential paperwork, follow up calls, an awesome idea I had for business but not pulling the trigger yet – these are all Radar items. I generally update my Radar once a week after I enter my current week *10s*. Remember, things need to earn the right to be on your list. It is tempting to loosen the red velvet rope policy on the Radar … don't.

This Week's *10s*

The Week's List of *10s* is my radar for *this week*. It is my commitment to this week. Nothing aspirational goes on this list. Anything that is not a *10* diffuses the energy and focus. I fill it in on Sunday night or Monday morning, and then move items over to Monday's *10s* list before I start the day. I love using my white board, however, if you are more mobile, and it works for you, your journal or phone app are also good ways to track *10s*. Personally, I want my Week's List as a reminder, but I do not want it cluttering my day. I set it and forget it – mentally and physically. The only thing constantly visible to me is my Today's List (see below). Much of the time, I have resistance to things that need to be done later in the week, so I won't be put on the calendar. (Earnest would put it on the calendar, but I know better.) My very organized assistant has tried to get me to practice "time blocking," where I schedule activities in my calendar, and then do them. It is the "and then do them," part I have trouble with. I am my own worst boss. But I am committed to my week's *10s* so when Thursday rolls around, I find the time to end the week … done.

[Update: Now, five years later I have a new tool to make time blocking effective, which I will explain in the "tools" section.]

Back to unscheduled This Week's *10s* List, paying bills that are due, booking a trip, and finally making the dentist appointment. I find it more effective to write it down – unscheduled -- than lie to myself with the "plan your week" exercise. For some reason, writing down the *10s* for the week, the things that I want to happen – or must happen with no specific commitment – also opens up my willingness to address the other things that must be done, *this week*, and *by me*, because of whatever *10* I have discovered about those tasks and actions. Remember, this is an experiment, but the goal is to keep you as free as possible.

Today's *10s*

– The Only List That Actually Matters

Today is all I have, today is all I can deal with, and today is the only day I can actually do anything anyway. The past doesn't exist and the should have been done yesterday lament is a waste of time and energy. My ex keeps a sign above her desk, "you are not behind, jump in where you are." The future is made up. You cannot do anything tomorrow, because it isn't tomorrow yet. In fact, it never is tomorrow. But you can think about, get overwhelmed and thwart today, worrying about tomorrow all day … today. My time and attention are my only commodities, and because all things on my list and in my head have equal urgency (and scream at the same volume), I make sure this list has that red velvet rope around it with a big burly bouncer standing guard. Only the elite may enter. The *10s* on Today's List are exciting to me for any number of reasons, but they all hold do-or-die energy. If they made it to today's list, I have already found the reason that even the most mundane actions reward me.

Guard today like a junkyard dog.

9.9s and below get chased out.

Those 9.9s may creep into he Week's List or the Radar, but they never make it to Today's List. If they do, and they show themselves, get them off. The relief is amazing. It does take time for your junkyard dog to learn their scent, but she will.

Working with the lists.

In this example, it's a Tuesday morning and I have set up my day. I love coming into my office after my workout and writing on my board. I sometimes do it the night before, but like I pack for a trip, it is as close to boarding time as possible. Almost always, a check mark goes next to Exercise and Meditate as I write the list, because they are *10s* and are usually done by this point in the day. It also gives me a feeling of satisfaction to check a couple of *10s* off before confronting the rest of them.

Radar	This Week's 10s	Today's 10s
Insurance Application (30th)	2 book chapters	Exercise
~~Dentist Appointment~~	Deposit to bank	Meditate
Call Pete Johnson	Client Invoices	John 8:30am
Return Lamp	Pay bills	Rich 11am
Meeting with Karen	Book CA trip	Zack Baseball 7pm
17 Lies books to clients.	Lunch - Mom	Mom Paperwork
Final edits to Stacy	Guitar	Bob Invoice
Follow up Max, Julie, Rich	~~Schedule Chris~~	Guitar 1 2 3
	~~Zack Baseball Tue~~	Call Chris
	~~Mom Paperwork~~	
	Schedule Dentist	

If you look at my Radar, you will see an assortment of things: the paperwork I don't really want to do but has a deadline, calls I really want to return, an idea I have for my clients, prospective conversations which I *want* to do, and other work that furthers my projects. Anything that I was able to schedule I did, and that is no longer on my Radar. As I add items to my Week or Today's List, I cross them off the prior list. I decided this is the week to schedule a dentist appointment, so it made it to the list (notice it's Tuesday and I still have not scheduled it, so you still see it on the week).

Remember, the Week's *10s* are inclusive of actions that fit the *10s* criteria but have no schedule. I always wait until the last minute to book trips. Last time it cost me $800 because of my habit of waiting, so this time I want to save that money. I feel the usual resistance to committing but I want that money more, so it made the list. I have no idea what day works to have lunch with my mother, but I know I want to do it, so it is on the week's list. The paperwork for my mother is daunting, and I don't want to do it, however the deadline is Wednesday and my *10* is avoiding the consequences (my mom missing out on a new apartment). It gets moved to Tuesday's list (with Chris and Zack) and all are crossed off the week's list. Tuesday is set now, with appointments, the things I want to do, and the things I hate to do, or always avoid doing, but want done for whatever underlying reason or consequence that makes them a *10*. Thanks to this practice and the freedom of my thinking, I can actually do those "not so fun tasks" without much drama these days. You will also notice that "Guitar" is on the Week's List *and* the Today List. It is a *10* for me to learn the guitar, and I want to practice three times a day to attain a goal I have set for myself. It stays on both lists.

Radar	This Week's 10s	Today's 10s
Insurance Application (30th)	2 book chapters	✓ Exercise
~~Dentist Appointment~~	~~Deposit to bank~~	✓ Meditate
Call Pete Johnson	~~Client Invoices~~	✓ Sarah 8:30am
Return Lamp	~~Pay bills~~	✓ 4PC 11am
Meeting with Karen	Book CA trip	○ Andy 3pm
17 Lies books to clients.	Lunch - Mom	✓ Send Completed Paperwork
Final edits to Stacy	Guitar	● Joe, Sarah Invoice
Follow up Max, Julie, Rich	~~Schedule Chris~~	● Pay Bills
	~~Zack Baseball Tue~~	○ Bank
	~~Mom Paperwork~~	Guitar ~~1 2~~ 3
	~~Schedule Dentist~~	● Date Night
		✓ Call Dentist
		● Write

In this illustration, it's now 1:30 p.m. on Wednesday. The Week's List is getting crossed off. There are items still on there. Some are in process, some I have resistance to, and some will get checked off at the end of the week when they get done.

In truth, I use lots of color on my white board, to make it fun and keep the practice from becoming monotonous. I'll spare you and only use two colors for consistency and my editor's sake, but I have 8 marker colors in reality. I can ignore important items in front of me if I want to, so using vivid color grabs my attention. Find a system that is fun and interesting to you. I have client who uses productivity apps with alarms and reminders. Some clients exclusively use their calendars and time blocking. Some write it down in their notebook. You must want to engage with your system. (And yes, there is a six-year old inside that is calling more shots than any of us wants to admit … but that is for the Mastering Midlife book, coming soon).

My morning appointments are checked off.

A few action items are checked off, and some have dots. I put a dot next to a task that I have done *some* work on, but is still waiting on either information or another action. They are not complete, but my mind will lie to itself and not see it on the board if I don't call attention to it. I do this also for a sense of momentum and satisfaction. The invoices are done, and just need to be sent. I have done 80% of my writing goal today. I paid some bills (the ones due tomorrow). Date night is scheduled.

The items with the circle are there to remind myself they are *still* there, and I have validated that they are *still* **10s**. If I leave them blank, they get lost. The doughnut hole is my recommitment ceremony to a **10**. I cannot say this enough, build a system you want to play with. Dots, smiley faces, gold stars, it doesn't matter. After five years, I see the people who build fun, interactive systems have long term success. Those who don't, still have success, but by resetting every few weeks. Both work … but the latter takes more energy.

By the time I shut down, the list gets acknowledged. I smile, and erase it. Sometimes I put the next day's list together, sometimes I don't.

What you don't see on the list is all the time I spent reading news, Facebook, looking at the fish in my koi pond, talking to friends on the phone, or generally not paying attention to my list. Some kind of strange time warp occurs. I still "waste" time, but with this consciousness, I snap back to what is deeply important more efficiently than I used to. I am miraculously productive without turning myself into an efficiency robot.

If you haven't guessed, I will be booking my California trip late in the day on Friday, because I absolutely have to put it off as long as possible, but I feel so exhilarated by completing my lists now that I will do it just to prove it was a *10*. I have come to hate "lying to myself."

Play with ways to keep track of your *10s*, make it your own.

This is not a system with rigid guidelines. It is only an illustration of how I keep myself honest – first to myself, and then to everyone else.

YOUR TOOLBOX

This practice itself is not that difficult. Figure out what you want to do, and do it. Pretty simple. It's your conditioned reactions and choices, the way you set up your relationships, as well as how you handle the obstacles life throws at you that will make the journey to taking back your time and attention more … interesting.

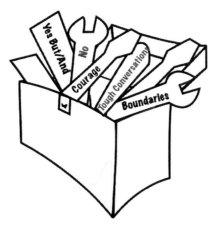

Freedom isn't free, as the saying goes. I'd love to tell you that the world, your boss and your loved ones will welcome your *10s* with open arms and a supportive demeanor. It is not that they don't support you, it's that they have their own *10s* … and we all fight for our own *10s*. As I journeyed this road, I found myself in unfamiliar territory, running into situations I hadn't anticipated. I had changed the game, and the rules for interacting with me, and the world responded. I needed to pick up new tools along the way if I was to take back the reins of my life.

COURAGE

You will need courage on this journey. I do not know where or when your "stuff" will come up, but it will. It may be a tough conversation, setting a boundary, or simply saying out loud, "I want to do this." It is different for everyone. When your feelings come up, it means you are doing this correctly. Those feelings are what kept you in the box. Stepping out is unfamiliar and you will need new muscles. Facing feelings is as courageous a thing as I have ever witnessed. It is where few tread.

For me, asking Earnest to leave the room, and not be the "nice guy" in every situation was like facing death. Just know that some resistance and obstacles will come up. Then know, sword in hand, you can and will face your demons – and you are always at choice to move forward when and if you want to. You can choose to back down or move ahead. Be kind to yourself, but choose. Watch your choices, and see what those choices reap. Trial and error alone will propel you ahead. You *cannot* fail.

RISK

I can promise very few things with this way of living, but I can promise that you will need to accept risk. As with courage, I am not sure where, but at some point, you will need to close your eyes and jump, without seeing where you'll land. It may be saying no to staying late at work, or showing your art for the first time, but it will feel like a risk. Whatever kept you in that box was keeping you safe. Again, anything outside that box is going to feel like danger. Go for it, or don't, but be aware of what each choice costs you or brings you. You *cannot* fail.

TOUGH CONVERSATIONS

Sometimes the only thing standing between me, and what I want, is a conversation I don't want to have. *I don't want to hurt his/her/their feelings. I'm embarrassed. I think he/she/they'll get angry. I'm being unreasonable.* Every conversation I didn't have, has been silenced by one of these thoughts or beliefs. Sometimes it is only this scary chatter that stands between me and my *10*. It's just fear. If I want something different, I need to stop and decide which is going to get to be that *10.* Tough conversations take courage and willingness to risk. Start small. Practice. You *cannot* fail.

TYPES of Difficult Conversations

Asking for help.

Asking for clarification.

Delegating.

Renegotiating.

Boundary management.

Creating agreements.

DIFFICULT CONVERSATIONS WORKSHEET

**Use the Difficult Conversations format to dive into the challenges
you are facing and what you need to overcome them.**

The challenge I'm facing is...

_____

_____

_____

The people I must speak with in order to resolve this challenge are...

_____

_____

_____

The difficult conversation I need to have is...

_____

_____

_____

The support I need to have this conversation is...

_____

_____

SAYING NO

It's true, "No" is a complete sentence. Use it. But sometimes an outright "no" is too harsh or could even be innapropriate. What we need is a beat to break free from the automatic reaction in order to know the more constructive response.

"Yes, but," is a good default response to cultivate. "I will do this for you, but I need _____in order to be able to accommodate your request."

This is a great way to negotiate your time and attention in a way that works for you. Again, often I don't know my answer right away, so my automatic response defaults to "Yes" – and I regret it later.

I got so tired of stumbling and fumbling with a boundary that I have gotten into the habit of answering, "I am not sure, may I get back to you?" Then I can do my inner work, phone a friend, gain clarity, and decide the best answer for me. I can still say yes. But now I have chosen.

Remember, you *cannot* fail.

BOUNDARIES

Good fences make great neighbors. Clear boundaries make for great relationships. Boundaries are the antidote to resentments. As I wrote earlier in the Truths section: nine times out of ten, if I am angry or carrying a resentment, it is usually because I didn't set a boundary.

In my workshops I assert, "If I have a resentment, it is because I haven't set a boundary, asked for what I want/need, or I am just a bit jealous." After some back and forth, I can usually get the participants to see the victimhood in resentment.

You can recognize the people in your life who set boundaries. Chances are, if you have a hard time setting them yourself, you judge those boundary-setting people pretty harshly, at least at first – but I bet you respect them too. The people you meet with the best boundaries are usually the ones living their *10s*.

I see three stages of boundary skills acquisition. I see them because this was my evolution … and then I watched these stages play out in CEOs, husbands, wives, and well, everyone who cares how people perceive them.

Level One (Full Earnest):

- Say yes to everything, run self into the ground
- create a full head of resentment steam
- Blow up and finally say ENOUGH!
- Set boundary in anger
- Low emotional intelligence
- Damaging to relationships
- Effective (with a nasty hangover)
- Lowers Respect

Level Two (Apologetic Earnest):

- Catch yourself being a doormat (and hate it)
- Find a line in the sand and get the courage to speak up
- Justify why you need to set the boundary
- Apologize for not living up to expectations
- Higher emotional intelligence
- Less jarring to relationships
- Effective (self-inflicted hangover because of new behavior)
- Few respect points

I love this level, though. It is where the recovering "people pleaser" allows their nervous system and communication skills to catch up with the new behavior. And they will. Be awkward and be proud.

Level Three (Earnest is gone):

- Set a clear boundary
- Ask for what you want
- Explanation only when needed for enrollment or for the relationship's sake

- Willingness to negotiate and create agreements
- Little or no hangover
- High emotional intelligence and leadership qualities
- Builds relationships and respect

The progression is amazing to experience and to observe. You will be surprised to hear people describe you as decisive, clear, and forthright. Some might even describe you as arrogant, but those are mostly people who cannot set boundaries. Always remember the tool of Love and Kindness (next section) and watch your leadership skills soar.

ASKING FOR HELP OR CLARITY

Of course, if you can find the answer yourself, do it. Show some initiative. But consider how much spinning your wheels unnecessarily costs you. I've heard all the excuses: I don't want to look dumb or lazy, I pride myself on being a self-starter, I don't want to bother anyone, and they are busy too.

This is where your commitment to the project is more important than saving face. If you cannot figure it out on your own, (or with YouTube), or it is just going to take valuable time away from the project, you need to ask for help. Remember it's not about you, it's about the project.

If you need help, resources, training, or more time ... ask. They can say no. Then you can decide if you want to go to bat for your ask, or find another way. If the "they" in this scenario are equally committed to the project and have respect for you, they will work on a solution. It may be a simple as someone has more experience and they can take ten minutes to save you and the project four hours. If you were the "they" wouldn't you want four hours saved if it could be done?

Expectations Vs. Agreements

Expectations	Agreements
▪ Often uncommunicated	▪ Creative
▪ Complaints = unmet expectations	▪ Relationship and co-authored
▪ Naturally rebellious	▪ Productive
▪ Disappointed or neutral outcome	▪ Communicates the gap
▪ Leads to frustration	▪ Basis for future negotiation
▪ Cowardly or lazy	▪ Courageous

We all walk around frustrated with unmet "expectations." We expect people to act a certain way, get something done, use directionals when they change lanes, and get our mocha chai soy latte done right. We expect things of our employees, spouses, kids, and bosses. Unfortunately, we walk around in a state of constant disappointment. Resentment. As the Godfather of Coaching, Steve Chandler would say,

"when you have an expectation, the best you can hope for is to come out even. You expect something and they do it. More often than not, they don't, so you are let down. If you drop all expectations, you spend your day delighted and surprised."

How do you feel and act when someone has an expectation of you? Human nature is to balk at pressure that is *put on us from someone else.* It is even more fun when the expectation was never verbalized, and you only found out afterwards.

Suffice to say, there is a better way. Create strong, clear, communicated agreements. I know I am more enthusiastic about a task or responsibility when I am involved in the creation of it. It takes extra time and effort … and it is the best way to neutralize a future resentment or misunderstanding.

This works in our personal lives as well. How often have you been angry at your partner because "they should know?" Has your teenager ever lived up to your expectation?

My kids had written agreements, *that they signed*, so the "alternative facts" of any given conversation could not be in disputed. And, this was when they were teenagers. They could be expected to break agreements … but had a tool for teaching and parenting.

I promise you, the more expectations you drop … the happier you will be.

The next time you send out a note saying roughly "I want this done, and I want it done by Friday," expecting it to be done, try this in writing or preferably in a conversation.

"I'd like this done and we need it to be done by Friday. Is this possible?"

"No, we have three projects that are also due by Friday (that you also said were urgent) and we do not have the staff to fill the fourth."

"Shoot, what do we need to do to make sure this is done? It *is* urgent."

"Tell me which of the other projects can be pushed, approve overtime for five people, or get me three more people from another department for a few days."

"Got it, I'll let you know how to proceed."

Now, Friday comes and we are all on the same page.

RENEGOTIATION

Renegotiation is an incredible tool. When an agreement deadline is coming up fast, and it's clear the objective will not be met … that is the time to pick up the phone. Burying our head in the sand is not a proactive strategy. By doing this you will:

- Let the person counting on the deadline know -in plenty of time- what is going to happen or not happen.
- Create trust and relationship
- Relieve pressure on yourself and your team from the unrealistic goal
- Probably come up with a creative way to an acceptable solution

Not keeping an agreement is unacceptable. But that doesn't mean you are in jail. Circumstances change. If you know you take agreements seriously, and that your word can be trusted, but something has changed to influence the situation, revisiting an agreement to keep it workable, is a difficult conversation that will benefit all concerned.

DELEGATING AND SUCCESS THROUGH OTHERS

Let's go a little farther with the example above. You will now need to produce, but it won't be by your own hands. It will be by your former co-workers. (More on that dynamic in a bit.)

You WILL want to show the team that you work as hard as they do.

You WILL want to feel busy and useful so you will take on too much.

You WILL fill your plate and your tasks will get squeezed.

You WILL freak out because nobody can do the work you were doing as well as you did it.

You WILL hate holding people accountable, criticizing their work, and pushing for excellence.

You WILL feel alone when you find out you are no longer part of the team but, one of "them."

It happens to every new leader no matter the level. You will need new skills and mindsets. You'll need to get your esteem from a different place. No worries … it doesn't need to take long, but your resistance to it will make it seem like a long time.

As you climb the ladder your contribution becomes increasingly strategic.

Every step up, you need to let go of something tactical that you did well and maybe even enjoyed.

Every step up the ladder you will feel less and less like you DO anything. Hint: the best leaders are never "busy."

Every step up the ladder your job will become more people focused.

Every step up the ladder you will need to sharpen your coaching skills.

Success through others means actually giving your team the tough, challenging, work.

It means critiquing that work when it comes back … both the awesome, and the not-so- awesome.

It means doing the above over and over until that person learns what they need to learn so the work is done to the standard you set.

It means, if you do any part of their work, you are selling them short.

THE FIRST 9.9 TOUGH CONVERSATION

Every so often, the resistance we feel to something that we *thought* was a *10* is trying to tell us something. The following story is an excerpt from a conversation I had with a colleague about resistance I was feeling. This talk had me concerned about letting people down, but as you will see, having the courage to open up a conversation about it paid off.

Me: "The Leadership Program, now that is also a *10*. It is so cool, and I love working with Stacy. The website is up, the concept is right on the money and people seem to be excited about it."

Colleague: "Has anyone signed up?"

Me: "No, but I'm having great conversations. Again, they lead to more one-on-one type ventures but everyone thinks it's interesting. Stacy is having trouble with enrollment also. We have the message and it is right on target. But…"

Colleague: "But what, Mark?"

Me: "F$#k! I really want to do it. But it is not like the book or my coaching business. Those are so clearly *10s*. Oh no, this is like a 9.9. I'm excited, I love the idea. I love the idea of partnering with Stacy. It would be so cool. But there is something missing. I know a *10*. Nothing will stop me when something is a *10*. This isn't like that."

Colleague: "Then you know what you need to do, Mark."

Me: "Oh no, I can't call Stacy and pull out of this. I just can't. I committed. I hate this. I do not like to back out of things and I really hate disappointing people."

The feelings of fear and shame were kicking my butt. I had no idea what to do with this.

Colleague: "What if you called her and were honest?"

Me: "Ugh. Not sure I have the guts to do it. Wait, I can tell her the truth. I really love working with you, love the idea, but it's not a *10* for me, at least not yet. I'd like to talk to you about how to make it a *10*. Okay, that I can do."

When I called Stacy and confessed my truth, she said "OMG, I am so with you. This isn't sticking at a *10* for me, either." Well, that was unexpected.

HOW AND WHEN TO SPEAK UP

I use my own life and my own state of mind and emotions as a laboratory. Once I learned that nothing, absolutely nothing, is happening "out there," the work to unravel my own jail cell could begin. And, I found that the answer to almost any problem was to speak up or take an action. Communication is a miracle. It brings the unseen to light. Not always, but often enough to improve most situations. If I consider someone's motivation is X, and that motivation (real or made up in my mind) angers me, I can ask and find out if it *is* X or something completely different. Nine times out of ten, it is something completely different and reasonable.

Action is another key to the cell block door. Often the feeling that our tires are stuck in mud is nothing more than our own thinking. By taking action, no matter how small or even right, we get ourselves out of the ditch and to higher ground.

So how do I know when to speak up or what to say when I do?

Let's play.

Speak up

Challenge	Possible Conversation
▪ Resentment?	▪ Boundary/Jealousy
▪ Overwhelm?	▪ Delegate, ask for...
▪ Can't say no?	▪ May I get back to you?
▪ Unmet expectation?	▪ Create an agreement
▪ Want something?	▪ Ask
▪ Didn't understand?	▪ Get clarification
▪ Fear?	▪ 5-4-3-2-1/Ask for support

SPEAK UP EXPERIMENT – HOW TO KNOW YOU NEED TO HAVE THAT DIFFICULT CONVERSATION OR TAKE AN ACTION.

For this experiment, I use a feeling or a thought as a trigger for communication or action.

RESENTMENT

If I feel a resentment (*Why did HE get a raise and I didn't?*) it is my cue that one of three things is going on:

1. I need to set a boundary.
2. I need to ask for something I want, or
3. I'm just jealous, such as jealous of their commitment and I need to look at the whole person or situation. (We can speak more about jealousy later.)

OVERWHELM

As a person with ADD overwhelm is my constant companion because I do not have the ability to separate things into A, B, and

C, or big rocks and small rocks. Everything on my list shouts at the same volume. That is why I need my *10s* list to be short and only those items that fit today's criteria to be visible. That said, overwhelm is about catastrophizing the future. It is bringing the consequences of not getting something done by some arbitrary or real deadline, into the present moment. This is where some deep belly breaths and clarity becomes essential. I cannot tell you how many times I have walked a client through a to-do list and it ends up almost empty, but they just couldn't see it for themself. Left their their own evaluation, everything has to get done, and get done now.

This is why looking at each item objectively is salvation.

Does it need to be done by me, by me now, or even at all. Should it be delegated? Do I need help? Do I just need to renegotiate the deadline?

Remember: Speaking up, for example, asking for help or renegotiating a deadline could mean "I'm not good enough" to your internal heckler. Walking past him or her is the actual breakthrough.

SAYING NO

You want to say no, but you can't. I mentioned earlier that once I realized I was a people pleaser who couldn't say no, and saw how that turned me into a resentment monster, I was forced to recognize that I'd need to utter that nasty word. I needed to learn to say that one-word sentence, and before I got comfortable with it, I opted to respond with, "May I get back to you?" This pause meant that I could still say yes, even just a few minutes later if I chose to, but I would be intentional about it. My inner lab rat wanted that pellet badly, craved the validation of saying yes. Sometimes it was agony not to. I needed to take the time to journal, or phone a friend to get perspective, just to muster a simple no. Programming is stubborn that way. But slowly, it became easier.

UNMET EXPECTATION?

Expectations are ridiculous and kill relationships. If I have an expectation of someone and they do not live up to that uncommunicated bar I have set for them, again, it can be a trigger for me. Crap, did I not have a conversation and create an agreement with that person? Were they clear on instructions, timeframe, quality of work? Did they verbally reflect what they understood to be the resulting action? If not, as a leader, as a friend, as a parent, as a partner, it's on me.

WANT SOMETHING?

This is "Sales 101" -- Did I ask for the sale? Of course, I'm being flip, but damn if that wasn't almost impossible for me to do. I'd have expectations, sure. Not communicated, not agreed upon, nothing ... so the result? I felt resentment. I could probably draw some fancy matrix to show how this is all a web of confusion that creates the jail cell, but I think you get the picture. The practice here ... get past that heckler and utter the words, "Would you be willing to ... or I want ..." Be prepared for a no (and a yes, which can be painful to the heckler – more later on that). We need to allow the no. Then, if it is important, Sales 102 is get willing to enroll.

DIDN'T UNDERSTAND?

Asking for clarity is another tough one on the ego. It is also one of the biggest causes of procrastination in me and in people I lead. YouTube has been a revelation. There is a reason it is the number two search engine (and why Google bought it). I can learn what the noise is in my washer, how to change a sim card in an iPhone, or create a dot art mandala. Same at work or home. Asking for clearer instructions, asking someone with more experience to show us something, will make the project go faster and be done better.

FEAR

Sometimes, we're just plain scared. Including all of the reasons I've written about above, and the hesitation to speak up, comes from some past hurt, or belief. Stepping past a lifelong inner threshold is tough, scary, and incredibly brave. Ask for help. Have someone hold your hand literally or virtually. Bookend. I have not been able to do any of this without support.

LOVE AND KINDNESS

The point of all these decisions is to live a full life, filled with the activities and people that we love. When saying no, setting a boundary, or having a tough conversation, love and kindness are always appropriate. At first, they may not be front and center. You may be awkward and unskilled. But over time, love and kindness become the tools to ground everything else. The more I treat myself with love and kindness, the easier it is to allow myself to focus on my true *10s*.

There is a difference between self-care and "being selfish." Once I put myself "on the list", love and kindness become my way of being in the world. Keeping love and kindness front and center, as guiding principles (after I flush the people-pleasing, a hollow cousin of real love and kindness), I can keep the *people* in my life a *10* while I also pursue what excites and inspires me.

WATCH OUT FOR THE 9.9s

The more I worked with this new insight, the more I learned about myself. I started to see more clearly the motivations under the desires. There were so many things on my plate that were compelling; things I wanted to do, sure, but they weren't things I was committed to doing. And therein lies the secret ingredient to a life of slogging and a life of rocket fuel. 9.9's had a lot going for them, but they were missing that last 1% … which was more potent than the other 99%. Commitment. An internal, "Hell yes."

Some of those motivations were internal, some were not. When the internal ones were clear, I was on fire. The external motivations were almost always based in feelings like fear and shame in some form, which put a kink in the flow. Earnest played a big part in creating 9.9s. He fell for the belief that I "should" want to do something. I should want … is not even close to a real want.

I looked back over my life. I thought of the things I had accomplished and the things I quit or things that never panned out. I started to see that anything that was a *10*, for whatever reason, I'd done. If it wasn't a *10*, I procrastinated, agonized over it, and beat myself over it. If it did get done, it happened the very day it became a *10* because of a deadline or a consequence I wanted to avoid.

Then it hit me.

I always do *10s*. I struggle with everything else.

When the person involved is a *10,* but the project still isn't, then a tough, vulnerable and honest conversation can change everything.

In tough conversations, if we are truthful, we can always leave the relationship in a better place. Of course, we cannot control other people's reactions. More often than not, though, we are a single tough, honest conversation away from feeling alive and free.

I keep a close watch on projects that get stuck in the mud. Whether it is my own resistance or what looks like outside forces, it means something is up. I can be excited and think I'm all in, but those pesky 9.9s that Earnest gets me into are life force killers. They show up when it is actually go time.

Sometimes I start something with enthusiasm and passion, and then I lose steam. Once I've checked on the real reasons for my steam loss and I conclude that something really isn't a *10* for me, I need to be willing to change course. Just because something looks cool, looks like the Universe is dropping it into my lap, doesn't mean it really is for me to do. If I start to notice resentments, or a secret hope that the project goes away, I am getting clues that it isn't a *10*. I will go down a wrong road with enthusiasm and excitement, but I need to be willing to cut the cord as soon as I get clear: it ain't a *10!*

WHEN MOM CAME TO TOWN

This book (the original ***Only 10s***) almost didn't come into being. I committed to a launch date, chose an editor and a publisher, told everyone in the world that I was writing it – and started. Awesome concepts hit the page. My life and business were firing on all cylinders. I was astounded at how my ADD magically disappeared, and my to-do lists were vanquished – one after the other.

I was scheduled to give a talk in front of my peers in Los Angeles, touting the discovery of how living the ***Only 10s*** life had been a *miracle*. I couldn't wait.

Then ... two weeks before the presentation ... my 83-year old mother came to town.

I actually had it all planned out. My mother could no longer live on her own in Florida, and needed to be in assisted living. I found an amazing place a few miles from my house, and it all seemed to be falling into place.

Did I mention, *I had this all planned out*?

I had no doubt the plans and systems I had in place were going to make this work like clockwork. I was great at setting boundaries, hiring help, delegating, and saying no, after all, right? I lived the principles in this book so well that I even hired an eldercare transition expert, to help my mother sort through her stuff, unpack, set up her apartment and move in. I so had this.

The day my mother moved in, the director of the facility mentioned something called "Transition Trauma." It happens to everyone, she said, it is unavoidable, and it passes. I scoffed at her prediction. I meditate. I set boundaries. I hire help. I am writing a book on all of this, afterall.

Please! I got this.

The moving truck breaks down, and is going to be a week late.

My mother is coming with so much stuff that the facility will not allow delivery, so it will all need to go into ... my garage!

My hired transition expert has a vacation planned, and now the delayed truck is coming the day after the expert leaves.

My mother arrives and moves in without her familiar belongings and calls me five times a day in a panic.

She has debilitating arthritis, and every action is difficult and painful. She is in a new place, without the essentials that help her get along (they are all on the truck), and more importantly, there is no HBO.

Cue the narration ... see both Mark and his alter ego Earnest making daily trips to Chesterfield. See them go to Wal-Mart, Target, and Bed Bath and Beyond for desperately needed supplies. Baseball games, tutors and regular parental duties are strained, but never fell off our list. (Earnest would never let that happen.) Earnest has shown up, and he can always run faster, do more and be everything to everyone. Earnest says, "Relax, I still got this."

A couple of days into my mother's move, we all get sick. I mean really sick. The coughing, chest pain, and weakness hit us like a ton of bricks. My mother, already weak and unsteady, is unable to care for herself. Not only are Earnest and I handling things heroically, we are doing so with a headwind. I hate to admit it but I am starting to crack. *I am not so sure I got this.*

This was transition trauma. And it is as bad as they had warned.

I am in hell. I do not have this. Resentments are everywhere. I am exhausted and feel like crap. I am sure I made the biggest mistake of my life. My mother is miserable and looking like she is going to die. We fight every day. I say things I can never take back. I want to burn all her belongings still in my garage. Boundaries are gasping for air. Fears flying. "Shoulds" are a way of life. I have failed.

And … what the hell am I going to talk about when I do this presentation? How the hell can I write a book when I hate every minute of my life? I really am a failure.

Soon, it was time for my business trip, and I was thankful for the break. My mother was miserable but stable, (and angry with me for leaving). The transition expert would be back from vacation, and ready to start dealing with my overflowing garage. My natural remedies were holding the illness to a manageable nuisance so I could function. I left for Los Angeles to give my presentation on "10s, Boundaries, Tough Conversations, etc." Panic fully set in as my presentation neared. Before I had been on fire, getting things done, creating like mad, setting boundaries, simplifying my life, and writing a book to be published quite soon. But since my mother had arrived, I hadn't done a thing on my own *10s* list! I was exhausted, and moreover, embarrassed.

I was a fraud and I had nothing to share.

Then, through prayer, meditation, and journaling, it dawned on me. I had it all wrong.

My mother was the *10*. Of course, she was.

Being a stand-up guy and a good son was a *10*.

She was ill, scared, disoriented, and things needed to be taken care of *now,* and *by me.* She was the very definition of a *10*. I had delegated and hired out all I could, but some things were just going to have to be me. I didn't *want* to do all these things, but I *did* want to be a good son and a responsible adult. I wanted my 83-year old mother to be comfortable and cared for.

I could choose this instead of being a victim.

Ironically, I'd been doing my *10* all along, but I was fighting it. I was being a victim instead of choosing it and owning it. It was indeed appropriate to put other *10s* aside, *for now*. My business trip was also a *10*, so when the time came, I got on the plane and trusted things would be handled while I was gone.

"And then my mother came to town," was the line that got the biggest laugh at my presentation. Of course, everyone could relate. We are high-achieving, kick-ass people who set our lives up the way we want them, and then, sometimes life just comes crashing in. We all have family, emergencies, and life circumstances that are out of our control. And, thanks G-d, we do.

My mother coming to town, transition trauma, and maturity, made my presentation, and this book, even better.

Note: as I update this five years later for **Only *10s* 2.0**, my mother has passed. And, this week, I am going to be interviewed by our guardian angel, Kelly Halteh, who held us when we moved in, and every day after, about this chapter and transition trauma. We are going to record it as a resource for all who are dealing with this most difficult time in life.

It is awesome to work on *10s* every day. I love creating my life and choosing where to focus my attention. But, it is when life comes calling in unexpected and overwhelming ways that practices develop which are useful during calmer times.

I learned many lessons from this time with my mother.

Sometimes the people I love just need me, my time, and my energy. Loving and being present is a *10.*

And sometimes it just has to be me who provides the care. Knowing the kind of person I want to be, who I choose to be, makes the *10* easy for me to spot even when the choice is difficult. When an emergency happens, I can confidently clear the decks, allow it to be a *10* – and dive in.

Dropping the resistance is half the battle.

With my mother, or any situation that I don't want to be happening, it is my anger *that it IS happening* which causes most of the pain. My lack of acceptance often makes it worse and drains my energy.

I can choose in any situation. I fell into victim role quickly with my mother's move, and forgot that I had a choice. I may not like the choices, but I still get to choose. Even when I only choose the path I hate the least, the choosing is empowering.

I get energy from knowing I decided to do it.

As Byron Katie says, "argue with reality, you only lose 100% of the time."

This shouldn't be happening is a losing battle.

Just because I can, doesn't mean I should.

At some point, Earnest needs to go, and I need to take care of myself. There are times and situations that become bottomless pits of need. No matter how much I give, it will not be enough. I can say no, even if I'm capable of doing something, and allow someone else, that person, or nobody to step up. I think of Oscar Schindler at the end of the movie, "Schindler's List": "This ring could have saved 25 more people." My inner Schindler will always feel guilty and believe I could have done more. When resentment creeps in, check your boundaries, perspective and self-care.

Boundaries, priorities, and the reins need to come back.

At some point, much sooner than Earnest would allow, it's done. My life, my *10s*, my priorities come back into play. It may be little by little, but they come back. People may get annoyed, disappointed, and still need, but they are more resourceful than it looks or they think they are. Put the white horse away and let them be their own hero.

Sometimes it just sucks.

Sometimes there is nothing I can do. If I am a caring, open person, life is going to get messy. Find joy, humor, and relationship where you can. Everything passes.

And yes, it's all a gift.

I am a better person, and this is a better book, because of transition trauma. It dug up all kinds of childhood patterns that I got the opportunity to work through. Quickly! We healed old wounds. My mother went through her own process, and figured out that she was responsible for her own well-being and happiness.

Note: I first wrote the story about my mother in 2015. Two and a half years after that she figured out her *10s*. Barely able to walk, and with few financial options, she found a way to move herself back to Florida. As dangerous and ill-conceived as the idea was, she was determined to live out her days exactly where and how she wanted. It was a *10* for her and she pulled it off. Shortly after she moved she was diagnosed with pancreatic cancer and passed away. Before she died, she thanked me for the years living close by getting to know her grandchildren and … told me she was glad to be dying as *she* wished.

I argued with her to move. I KNEW it was wrong. It placed untold burden on me. And, I am grateful, in hindsight, as I write this … that she stood for her *10*.

FINDING THE INNER COMPASS

"Mark, if I were in a foxhole, surrounded by the enemy, I would want you by my side. I know that you would get us all out to safety, without question. But if I were headed into a peacekeeping mission, I would leave you at home. I'm not sure you are done with the addiction to excitement. That is why I am not sure I want to work with you."

This was my first conversation with my coach, Rich Litvin. What a blow. I thought of myself as a new age, peace-loving man who would like nothing better than building new housing for homeless refugees, *on a peacekeeping mission*. But I knew Rich was right. I would build two houses and be off doing something else more interesting. I love the fight, I love shiny objects, I love the juice.

What I have learned since writing this passage in the original text is that the "fear of the blank page" is real. Many of the ancient sages say that humans busy themselves through life by creating problems and then solving them. I had come to learn, before writing this book, that I was afraid of my own creative energy. I was afraid of using my voice. That fear was so great, I needed to create distractions to keep me to busy to face empty, free time.

The truth was, my compass was broken. My day consisted of the search for a dopamine rush or, if I was hunkered down to accomplish something important, waiting for something shiny to walk by so I'd have an excuse to leave my boring task. If my projects weren't providing the interest, a friend in a crisis would do the trick. And hey, I was helping someone.

Ritalin helped. But only if I sat myself down, decided what to do, and got to work. If I didn't have a plan, I just focused harder on the news, Facebook, or researching a new iPhone. I had to steer the ship in the direction I wanted *before* I took the pill. Especially, if what I was starting was mundane. If it was interesting, but frustrating, I would bounce off the second something else distracted me.

This brings me back to the conversation with Rich in 2015, about following my energy. My fear was that I would follow this ADD excitement junkie part of myself over a cliff, because the view was cool. In reality, something different showed up. Instead of beating myself up for not *wanting* to do something that seemed important, I paid attention. Instead of doing something I didn't want to do, I asked more questions. I learned that often, fear (or terror) was actually excitement. The most frightening time of sky diving is at the door of the plane, once you jump … "Wheeeeeeee."

Why am I doing this? Why am I not doing this? What is really going on?

In the weeks after the conversation with Rich, I unpacked every action item that came my way. I did the same for my clients. I would go through our to-do lists and ask questions. We would get mindful of what was behind every demand on our time and attention. Something cool was happening to my clients and me.

The more conscious we are about *the why* of our actions, the more we are able to see <u>choice</u>.

With choice comes freedom. More often than not, the task itself holds very little charge. It is the underlying fears and beliefs about those tasks that hold all the information. The *10s* in each situation will reveal themselves.

I would rather do this than have a difficult conversation. (Oh, I'll just do it.)

I would rather lie to myself than admit that I am afraid. (I didn't really want to dance.)

I would rather make them think better of me than say no. (I'll get praise if I volunteer.)

I would rather avoid fear than speak, act, choose, or risk. (I'd just embarrass myself anyway.)

On and on, the underlying motivations clouded what I really thought about any given request or my own wants. It was a magnetic storm that messes with our internal compass.

Client: "Mark, I am so stressed this week. We are overwhelmed with projects and I am short staffed. The CEO wants it done by Friday, and I just can't do it. I need to quit, I've had it with this stress and unrealistic expectations." (Fight or flight – no creative thinking)

Me: "What needs to happen to relieve your stress so you don't just quit?"

Client: "I don't know." (false confusion)

Me: "What would you do if you were bold, fearless, and willing to risk looking bad?" (release the tension)

The client takes a deep breath, and says "That's easy, I would have a conversation with the CEO to adjust expectations or get more resources. Oh, I see where you are going ..."

Now we have clarity. Now we know the confusion was a fog to hide the fear of having that difficult conversation.

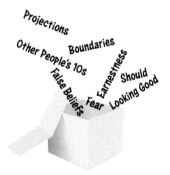

Unpacking and examining each item on the to-do list takes work. In fact, it is stressful and time consuming, *at first*. After a few days, it will get easier, and your choices clearer. Once you see the fear, the "shoulds," and the projection, it will be easier to get clear on the next right action. You may take on a task to avoid a consequence, but at least you will know why you are doing so and choose. Confusion lessened for me, and it will for you also.

The same becomes true for the shiny objects. As I write what YOU should do, I have fun little wants. Let's go through my crazy brain a bit.

I want a fish tank. My koi pond is full, and I am banned from buying more fish. I go by the pet shop and look at the miniature sharks, and I can visualize the tank in my office. We have already established that I generally do what I want, and buy what I want, when I want it. But focusing on only *10s* has ruined much of my random dopamine chasing, at least for shopping. The fish tank is an 8. Distracting myself from the work of the three projects I say are *10s* is a 9. The projects are, in fact, the *10s*. The fish tank doesn't fit. The little kid in me whines about it, but the adult, who does only *10s*, knows the choice. The time and attention it consumes will take me away from what is really important to me. I grumble, but I choose.

**You are reading this book instead of
scrolling through Netflix, so the *10* won.**

The same happens with my car addiction. There's nothing shinier than a new car and I got into the habit of having a new one every two years. Please save your judgement. I know. I recently traded in my convertible for a very luxurious, and awesome, small SUV. Turned out to be the best car I have ever owned. When I purchased the Sonic Blue Lexus Convertible, it had all the ingredients I longed for. Flashy, fun, and my favorite color. It also filled the need to finally "put myself on the list." It actually was a *10*. I needed to do something for myself at that time. But it had served its purpose and was no longer useful. My heart tugged as I thought about trading it in ... but, the sun was out ... Then I thought about the white seats, and no trunk. I saw my priorities and what would support my life, and how my two big dogs can jump in the back. My elderly mother and her wheel chair could get easily get in and out. I could go to Home Depot and throw stuff in my little truck. I blazed through the snow in it whereas the Lexus couldn't leave the garage. Shiny object (convertible) was now seen for what it is. Nothing wrong with fun. But I needed practical. Not as fun, but me and my dogs thrived when the compass point was clear.

Original text from five years ago:

> "I never pass on a new Apple product. Apple watch! I want one, gotta have one.
>
> I will look so cool. Oh wait, my wrist buzzes every 30 seconds. I'll also need to charge it, set it up, and pay attention to it. Yup, just a distraction. This is a small, unnoticed miracle the world missed, but for me, freedom.
>
> This is how I find my compass every time it gets lost. The more I use my to-do list as a practice in why I am spending my precious time and attention on anything, the clearer I see where my compass is pointing.
>
> The more I slow down and look at my impulses, I can see what I am really wanting."

In the five years of living and teaching this methodology for clarity, I have cringed at the above passage. What was agony for me -- passing on the fish tank and the new Apple product, is now how I operate. My inner child gets in line more easily. The emotional intelligence in each decision has grown to be the default. Yes, I get distracted by shiny objects, but the struggle and choice take less of my psychic energy.

And in five years of coaching and teaching, I've seen it have that effect on everyone who practices it. That clarity is a game changer in business, life … and fulfillment. It starts with the small choices, in the here and now. Wrestle with your distraction. Meet the disgruntled little kid inside that wants what he/she/they always wanted. Make friends and over time … gain freedom.

Once you find your compass, and honor its direction in your life, living your values becomes simpler. Decisions and choices become clearer.

Now you are ready for the big *10*.

FINDING TRUE NORTH
THE ULTIMATE *10*

In *Only 10s 2.0*, I considered leaving this section out. While I found the practice profound and used it in my coaching regularly I also started forgetting about it until a reader or a client would remind me by talking about a powerful new insight.

Such as when my then 20-year old son reread *Only 10s* and said, "I figured out my True North."

"What?" I had forgotten about this section, again.

"I know what my *10* is for this year and it is learning about myself. I am going to take a year to learn who I am and what I really want, and every choice I make either fits or doesn't. Everything I do this year will be for this one goal." He continued, "My plan is to go to Israel and yeshiva (Orthodox Jewish seminary) and learn about myself through my love of Judaism. But if I cannot go because of COVID-19, whatever I do here will be for that goal. I can go to

Northern VA Community College and take online classes and still achieve what I want."

I was blown away. Life in 2020 was precarious and unpredictable, but he had a clear, values-based path that would guide him through the uncertainty. He told me that I needed to keep this section in the book, echoing what I'd heard from so many clients and readers.

"Dad, I got into yeshiva and they approved my visa. I have a flight next week."

"But everything is shut down, they're not letting anyone from the US in."

"I know, its kind of a miracle. They're letting our group in, and we just have to quarantine for two weeks."

"Dude, you financed this, you planned it, you got scholarships, you even manifested a plane when there are none. That was a powerful *10*. Nothing stopped you. I'm in awe."

So there you go! If Jake can manifest a travel visa in 2020, using this exercise, there is nothing out of your reach.

When it comes to *10s*, trusting my attention and my enthusiasm became essential for daily momentum. As I teased out the False *10s* and learned to zero in on my inner compass, I started getting things done at a rate I had never experienced. I built a successful coaching practice, speaking career, valuable workshops, a top-tier podcast (with over 250 episodes), marriage, new home, launched my kids, and I'll be writing two new books after this one you are reading.

PPhheewww.

Focused *Only 10s* is rocket fuel.

Now that I was freed, my mind went back to the big projects, goals, and dreams I had discounted because of ADD and not trusting myself to follow through.

The energy that was tied up in fear and hypervigilance of responsibility, was released for creative and generative thinking. No longer beholden to beliefs that are not true, my white board filled with new ventures to pursue. I was excited about everything.

Then I thought of the Mark Zuckerberg and the "One Goal" story. What was my one goal? I had no idea. Whenever I want to figure something out, I head to the white board. I have an entire wall covered with enough whiteboard real estate to spread out and let my mind wander in all directions. My clients are also thrilled with the added space. I recommend the biggest, baddest whiteboard you can bring into your life.

I wrote down my current projects and started asking questions of myself. I tried to capture the exact process I took myself through.

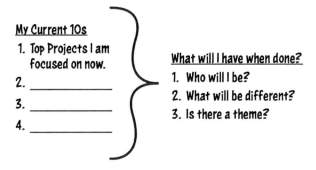

So when I actually accomplish these *10s*, what does that mean? More importantly, how will life be different, how will I be different? What is the thread that ties them together? Remember, the *10* is *almost always* the reward, the avoidance of consequence, or a desired feeling or state (accomplishment, safety, fulfillment).

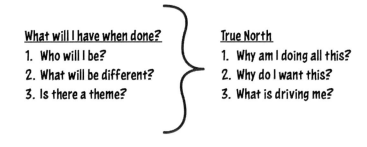

Like any good coach, I kept asking myself questions. My favorite coaching question is a simple, "So?" It's my shorthand for longer questions like, So what? Why do you want to be this person, have this outcome? What is driving you? What is the deeper *10*? I turned those questions on myself. Now I was getting somewhere. The projects feed into my feeling a certain way, looking a certain way, or having something Id want. Once I felt this or had that, would that the end? What did I ultimately want?

True North
1. Why am I doing all this?
2. Why do I want this?
3. What is driving me?

My 1 Goal/Vision
1. This is where I am headed
2. All else needs to fit into this context

My son Jake had one goal, "to learn about himself." Everything needed to fit that value. If we work backward, Mark Zuckerberg's one goal was to "Grow Facebook." Why? What was his True North? I have no idea why his one goal was to grow Facebook (and now in 2020, we question if its growth was a positive thing or not), but something was driving it.

Let's go back to our original list of projects and ask some questions.

Why are they 10s?
1. Do each fit in the context of True North?
2. For each, are they on purpose?
3. Are they really 10s?

Now that we have more clarity on our motives, what we want, and how that leads to our Ultimate *10* or One Goal, we can question our projects individually. *Why* are they a *10*? Sometimes one or two are on the list because we *want* to do them. If they excite me, and are not deemed a distraction, with my newly accurate compass, then they stay and I continue questioning the list.

Do these projects fit into the context of what I actually want for my life? Is it a *10* ... or is it an 8 or 9 taking me off of my true north?

If they pass the questioning, they stay.

If not, they come off the list.

I still may do them, but that is not the point.

If a new hobby, say, skydiving is on the list but does not fit, we can still go skydiving. If it is a *10,* it will end up being scheduled without much coaxing. But it is not something to keep front and center, because now we have our eye on the ultimate prize.

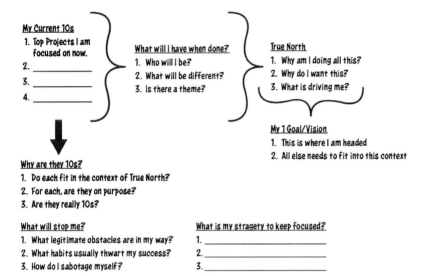

My Current 10s
1. Top Projects I am focused on now.
2. _____
3. _____
4. _____

What will I have when done?
1. Who will I be?
2. What will be different?
3. Is there a theme?

True North
1. Why am I doing all this?
2. Why do I want this?
3. What is driving me?

My 1 Goal/Vision
1. This is where I am headed
2. All else needs to fit into this context

Why are they 10s?
1. Do each fit in the context of True North?
2. For each, are they on purpose?
3. Are they really 10s?

What will stop me?
1. What legitimate obstacles are in my way?
2. What habits usually thwart my success?
3. How do I sabotage myself?

What is my stragety to keep focused?
1. _____
2. _____
3. _____

Let's look at the whole.

The beauty of this exercise is that I can talk a client through any section we start with and expand outward. They may know their ultimate goal is to build a company or to leave a legacy. We can work backwards to create projects (and check those in progress) that will support that outcome. Along the way, we will shore up his/her/their why and his/her/their drive to do so, drowning out any distractions.

After I questioned my projects, my motives and found my ultimate goal, I was curious as to what would stop me. I knew my shortcomings well (and you should too after reading much of this book), so I listed them out. Then I asked, how will I keep these known potholes from becoming a problem? I anticipated the stumbling blocks, and created strategies for staying on track in spite of them.

Get out a piece of paper or go to your own whiteboard, and start answering the questions and let yourself wander through your own mind. A mere 15 to 30 minutes later, you'll be amazed at the insights.

For me, (the easily distracted), having a bright intense star to shoot for is the best anti-glare tool for the myriad shiny objects that call from the side of the road.

It's called a BHAG – Big Hairy Audacious Goal.

Take it from me (and Jake), it's a great way to live.

RESISTANCE AND THE *10*

I'm sitting here with my heart in my mouth, and my brain all in a fog. I want to go to Facebook, the news, eat something, or find anything at all to do besides write this chapter. What chapter? I don't even know what to write. It's painful, and I hate this feeling. Maybe this isn't a **10**. *Maybe I'm a fraud.*

Stephen Pressfield calls that garden variety "resistance" in his masterpiece, *The War of Art.*

My psychiatrist would call it ADD.

My Enneagram type says it is part of my personality: Sevens feel "trapped" by any task or commitment.

All I know is that I am battling between something I really seem to want to do, and wanting to relieve this tight, anxious feeling at any cost. It has been a 50-year battle to date. I've been very successful in business and life. However, I have also made my way through school, jobs, and almost everything by using shortcuts and hacks. When the stakes are high enough I always find a way. If the stakes are not high enough, I walk away. It is a creative way to live, and the gold is that I've learned to be very resourceful. This is a topic in my forthcoming book, *Mastering Midlife.* But navigating the shortcomings of my personality, and wrestling with that pain (real or imagined) used to leave me fatigued by the daily battle. I'd reach incredible heights, only to crash and burn, and need to reset.

How many things have I started only to walk away? How many things sit half done? How many ideas pop into my head that excite me only to fade as quickly as they appeared? I've had enough. I will no longer live this way. I will sit at this keyboard until something happens. I will type crap if that is all I have, but I will type.

I put my hands on the keyboard.

It's been 20 minutes. I just keep moving. I started by bouncing around the pages like a beach ball, writing, and rewriting random paragraphs – and now I am actually finishing a chapter. The lump in my chest is gone. I am flowing. I feel like I took a Ritalin, but I haven't. I have a meeting in 30 minutes that I wish wasn't scheduled now, because I want to keep working. This is awesome, but how did it happen? Where did the flow come from and where did the resistance go?

The desire to write this book outweighed the feelings by just enough to keep me going. Writing was a **10**, so avoiding those feelings (no matter how painful) dropped to a 9. Like any muscle or habit, I am learning to work through the feelings and fog. But only because writing this book is a **10**.

I have spent a lifetime avoiding the feelings (and giving in to them) that I associate with certain types of work. I trained myself day after day, year after year. My habit or conditioning is to reach for relief.

In the years I have been coaching I've seen that same conditioning show up with different flavors in my clients:

- Create and focus on fires all day and never get to important work.
- The hero complex: fixing everyone else's work.
- Finish every to-do list and leave no time for self-care or relationship.
- Do the things that should be delegated to avoid the intangible strategic planning needed.

Take a few minutes.

What do you avoid that you know lights a fire, but you never have time for? What would bring so much value to the organization but you just can't get to it? What one thing, today ... big or small, that if you did it, would have the biggest impact?

Write it down.

Now ... what do you need to do, to make the time?

What conversation do you need to have?

What needs to go undone to make room for what needs to be done? Write it down.

Chances are, the above brings to mind fears or excuses that it's a bad idea. Write it down.

What support do you need? (Remember tools and difficult conversations?)

Are you committed? If so, by when will you do this?

Resistance is real. It's painful, but it's no match for a _10_.

I have a confession to make. I used much of what I write about in this book to *actually write this book.* I was working on a big visible project for the following month, my mother called several times a day, we are readying my son for college, my website needed updating, I needed to change my insurance, and they all wanted my attention. But most of these tasks were not on my (then) Summer 2015 _10s_ List.

Summer 10s
Finish iCoach Book
Only 10s book
PC Intensive Project

You will notice only three items on this list. Although the other items I listed are important and took up quite a bit of my time and attention, they happened automatically. I could trust that they would make themselves _10s_ on their own each week. My three projects would not. I needed to deliberately and consciously carve out time to sustain them. I needed to set boundaries, work through obstacles, resistance, and failure to bring them into reality. "Automatic" does not apply to creative endeavors.

If you are reading this book, you know it was a real **10** for me. (And again, it is a **10** in summer of 2020 amid COVID-19, social unrest, economic devastation and a political firestorm). You will also know that fear, resistance, tough conversations, and everything else that might have stopped this book from coming into reality, were pushed from the top spot.

In my life, a *10* is *the* royal flush that beats any hand.

Since having this awakening, walking through resistance has been a practice for me. It is a muscle I work and a habit I feed. Leaning into fear, allowing myself to be uncomfortable, and walking through the dreaded fog, is no longer the thing to be avoided at all costs. It is the compass pointing towards things very worthwhile. Getting up and going down to my basement gym at 5:30 a.m. sucks. But, because I want to fit into my Hugo Boss fitted shirts and be healthy when I meet my grandchildren, down I go.

Because I want to create my life, I am willing to do the conscious and often difficult work on *these* muscles as well.

What if my *10* doesn't fit my current situation?

One of my clients, who also suffers with ADD and is blessed with a healthy attraction to all things music and art, worked diligently to fit into the corporate world. Now a successful vice president of business development at a leading marketing agency, he walled off his passions that didn't seem to align with his day-to-day responsibilities. After working together for a while "to fix the stress of being a model corporate citizen," it became clear that his passions were pulling at him every day.

So, we explored his list of current (important) projects, and also the projects he longed to work on. He showed clear energy in several directions that (at first) didn't fit into his job description. As he learned to trust his internal compass, he found creative ways to not only bring his love of music and art into his corporate world, but to do so in a way that would differentiate his firm.

He shared this experience with me.

> *"I often dreamed about a career in the music business, but chose the marketing and ad agency route instead. Though I dabbled in music, I was never really able to create a way to satisfy my passion for the arts. I was good at my job, successful and making money, but something was missing.*

> *Many years later, I found myself in a unique position to build a bridge between these two worlds by developing a platform that celebrates collaboration between brand marketers and the music business. It turned out their interests were increasingly aligning, and many of them didn't know how to capitalize. My vision was to develop an event series that would tour the country, bringing these interests together for a combination of networking, panels and industry learning, and live music performances.*

> *My mind said it would be too difficult finding venues in every city, nobody would show up, someone else must be doing this already, my colleagues will wonder if this is a good use of my time and whether it aligned with the company goals.*

> *Despite all the questions and insecurities, I knew I was on to something unique. There was a need in the market. It was unquestionably my passion, my 10, and I knew I was the one to create it.*

> *I sold the vision to the executive team at my company and got to work.*

> *The tour is off to a great start and the response has been more enthusiastic than anticipated. I learned that once I commit to something I completely and passionately believe in, things begin to fall into place.*

I took a risk and followed where my energy and enthusiasm took me, and the result has opened up my career, a differentiation for my company, and brought my greatest passion into the mix."

Fast forward five years from the telling of this story. Eventually my client's passions, and the increasingly conservative focus of the company he helped build, were separated by an insurmountable divide. The corporate world was no longer a *10*. My client was more and more committed to his passions and vision. He took the terrifying step to part ways with his own past success, to see where his *10* could take him. In other words, he went out on his own.

Following this path can be messy. In an interview, Brene Brown was asked about the reason for her new book *Rising Strong*. She said that after *Daring Greatly*, which challenged people to risk and "get in the arena," she got a lot of mail. People told her they had *dared greatly*, and failed. They were glad they did, but now what?

We celebrate people who follow a passion and set out on their own, when they succeed. Rarely do we see the pain involved in the choice, and the bumps and bruises that are inevitable along the way. If they fail, we pretty much roast them for being selfish, misguided, or conclude they must not have been as talented as we thought they were. Amplify that by 1000 for the negative nature of the internal talk when success doesn't follow a huge leap.

I related to my client … I had done exactly the same thing when I decided to "be a coach." My former boss used to text me occasionally and ask, "Making as much money as you did here?"

I call this no-mans-land. That perilous time between cutting the ties and the first successes of a new direction. You can almost taste that fear when you imagine taking this step, can't you? It's real, and it can be worse than you imagined. Never, ever take this step without support. Is it worth it? An irrefutable, "Hell Yes." And there are also sound reasons for staying safely on the shore. Knowing the shore wasn't actually safe either is a subject for *Mastering Midlife* … but for now, let me say this -- the metaphor works.

Here is a summary of the five years that followed his leap looked like for my client.

- Got married and became self-employed. Many difficult intimate conversations here.

- Wrote a book he was not sure he could write, or anyone would care about.

- Took consulting gigs to keep up the cash flow.

- Placed small bets on different projects to see which ones would pan out.

- Watched money fly out the door, had creative but not financial successes, questioned everything, daily. Felt feelings, dealt with crippling self-doubt, risk, growth, learned new skills, and kept walking.

- Finally found "the thing," and threw himself entirely into it. Commitment.

- Continued to question everything, daily.

- Created a partnership, landed a dream deal, and finally got validated that this was the *10* he was looking for.

Too often, the people who come to me for coaching have put themselves into a box that they think will keep them safe. They follow the rules, and they make themselves into the people they think they need to be to get ahead. To do this they must shut off a piece of themselves, the very part that makes them creative, unique and energized.

I did it myself for years. And it was the right choice at the time and for my responsibilities. Everything I did up to the point I made the decision to change, enriched the next chapter of my life. My coaching is infinitely more valuable to the people I serve because I made it in the corporate world. My client went into his new venture with the business acumen, negotiation, and sales skills that were invaluable to his new partnership.

I never discount the past. Or timing.

Of course, it is risky to color outside the lines, to speak up, to offer outrageous ideas, but those who do experience leap frogging, incremental success. Passionate, alive people give a company (that wants them) lifeblood. Those that don't will crush that creativity.

It is up to you whether you want to nurture your own, or continue to cram yourself into the box.

My client's story started simply. In our first conversation, I asked him to practice piano five minutes every day. For me, I started a coaching course to make me a better salesman and dad. That worked for me. That's it.

Baby steps.

What baby step can you take, today?

QUESTIONS, STATEMENTS, AND ANSWERS

So what about all the little stuff, the 3s, 4s, and 5s?

They all go. They all get off your *10s* list. If a 4 or 5 crops up and you really want to do it, then it becomes a *10*. If you do drop it out, it was never important. You do not have time or space for these things. If they were that important or that fun, they would be a *10*. Get it? If it is a 3 today but you know it is going to be a *10* sometime in the future, it belongs on the calendar or the Radar list instead. You can always do things that are less than a *10*, but only AFTER your Today's *10s*.

Until then, keep them off your visible list!

That's the trick … see your *10s* and only your *10s*.

After your *10s*, it's all fair game.

Waste time, watch a show, doodle, do a few 3s. Just do your *10s* first.

What if I hate my job, do I still have to go to work?

No, you don't. You don't HAVE to do anything. It is the lie of the victim. You want to eat. You want to support the people you love. You want health insurance. You do not *have* to go. The *10* is what the job provides.

Choose!

Hate this job? What are you doing to get another one? You choose to go to work because you do not want the consequences of not showing up more than you do not want to go. It still may suck, I get it, but you are not a victim here.

Choose, change, act, but never allow yourself to be helpless.

Perspective changes everything.

What do I do when my lists are getting too long?

I love this one. I got so good at getting my lists done I put more and more on the *10* list. Soon it was a conventional to-do list, and my *10* was the satisfaction at the end of the day of seeing all those check marks. But that didn't last long.

I have no passion for completed lists. Some achievers do, and the risk here again is dilution. Remember, the original tagline for this book is "get the right things done," not "getting lots of things done."

It is easy to reset. When the list starts looking long and uninspiring, take a break, go through the qualifier process, and ruthlessly cut it down.

What about all my obligations that are taking up my time?

We all have obligations pulling at us. I have two sons and an aged mother to care for. I have bills to pay, and retirement to save for. The question is whether they own the strings to my arms, legs and mind ... or do I? It takes courage to look honestly at where I am allowing circumstance to dictate my priorities or my feelings. It takes courage to set a boundary, and take time for myself. It takes *risk* to say no. It takes *worth* to put myself on the list.

I will say it again and again, perspective changes everything. Moving from the victim of circumstance to the owner of your experience seems like a mind game … but it is an energetic shift that impacts your outside world in miraculous ways.

Move "I have obligations," to "I am blessed with responsibilities I have chosen," and see what happens. Then set those boundaries.

I heard a story at a seminar addressing the specific needs of overworked women, that I applied to my own life, (with great difficulty at first). It has paid off in unexpected ways.

Women often give and give until their teacup is empty. Then they try and steal a little time to fill the cup again. Over and over, they give to their families and jobs from an empty cup. We suggest a better strategy, fill the cup first. Fill it until it is overflowing, and give from the saucer, the overflow. When you give from this place, it is abundant and loving, and infinite.

I was a better father when I took time to go to the gym or took Tuesday nights for my men's group. I was a better father when I had my own projects and passions. I showed my kids, by example, how to be a full, happy adult. My spouse found me more attractive, because I was interesting and alive. Of course, I did not do these things at their expense. But I did tell the truth to myself, let go of Earnest, and find a more balanced approach. I was shocked to find out my kids were fine if I only got to half their baseball games.

In Episode 23 from the Mastering Midlife Podcast, "Build an Interesting Personal Life, Add Rocket Fuel to your Career" I interviewed a former workaholic Uneeb Khan, and he talked about how his maniacal work ethic never got him promoted. When he started exploring his interests and volunteering, the promotions and accolades started pouring in.

Bottom line: Live a life while you are living your life.

Thank me later.

A CALL TO ACTION

When my clients, who often seem to "have it all," break character and get honest about their lives, there is a common experience. They all seem to long for something that feels lost to them. They are sheepish to admit that they want something more and are embarrassed to be "ungrateful" for all the blessings in their lives.

"I have it all," they say, "it's selfish to want more."

I don't think it is *more* they want at all.

It is easy to cut away false ambition driven by false beliefs of fear, but not so easy to face what is left. The blank page, or free time, can be more overwhelming than a jam packed schedule. And, I often find that the things they are looking for are what is hidden in the "what's left." I help them with the courage to look.

If I am not striving, proving myself, keeping up an image, what's left?

I think the most difficult thing of all in modern society is to let go of the marketing, the "shoulds," and the fears of being left out.

It's frightening to stop the noise and ask: "Who am I, and what do I want?"

The first time I ask a new client these questions the answer is always "less stress or pressure." Always.

But as we unpack this response it becomes clear that most of the pressure is indeed self-inflicted. It doesn't come from "out there," it's an inside job. Yes, there are responsibilities and demands, but the stress part is optional. It is not easy to let go of being a victim (or outrage) to see our own part in creating what we *don't* want, but it is the only rewarding way forward.

Are you really too busy firefighting to do *Only 10s?*

As I call you to action below, your brain is going to go nuts. *How am I going to get to prioritizing when every day is like a firehose of things to react to?* And that's legitimate. Here is a little story.

A man is walking near a river and hears screams for help coming from the water. He sees people floating down the river, struggling, and going under. He jumps in and starts pulling the people out. Another man is walking by and the first man yells to him asking for assistance. To his shock, the man runs away.

After a while there are no more people coming down steam, so weary and wet he gets back on his journey. After a while he sees his runner and asks, "I yelled for help, people were drowning, why did you run away?" The man said, "I ran upstream to stop them from falling into the river."

So no matter how hard it seems, if you want to get out of the constant firefighting that is killing your creativity, then find a way to get upstream. The short term pain WILL pay dividends.

Just because you don't want to see it, doesn't mean it isn't true.

We are the authors of our lives. There are scenes and characters that populate this world, but we wrote many of them with our past choices. Yes, unexpected obstacles or misfortunes may come our way, but for the most part, if we look back, we can see what led us to exactly where we are at this moment – the choices we mad or didn't make.

Once we see this, the door to freedom is opened.

My challenge to you is simple.

Are you willing to put the work in to find out what you want?

Are you willing to strip away the facade that masks who you are and speak your truth?

Are you willing to matter, *really matter?* To put yourself on your own list?

How often have we learned that an ounce of discomfort now, will relieve a pound of pain later? I can promise you, though uncomfortable at times, the work is worth it.

MASTERING MIDLIFE
(THE NEXT STEP)

The premise of my keynote speech, podcast, and forthcoming book, "*Mastering Midlife – How to thrive when the world asks the most of you*" is this:

The drives and motivations that pushed us to success in our 20s and 30s often wane or even turn on us in our 40s and 50s.

Midlife Crisis is not inevitable, it is the consequence of not evolving ...

of ignoring that still small voice inside us that can't be heard over the noise.

We need to slow down and listen.

Only 10s and the consciousness that it forces us to adopt is the first step to listening to what life wants to tell us.

Remember that all we own is our time and attention.

Our lives are built by the daily choices of where we put our attention and how we spend our time. Simply looking at a to-do list, unpacking what is there for us to learn about ourselves, our joys, our avoidance, and our patterns – and being willing to try anew – is a great place to start.

This is a journey that opened up a whole new world for me. Universes actually.

Yes, I get my list done each day, (and that is a miracle in and of itself), but I have received so much more from this simple exercise. Allowing only *10s* in my life, trusting my real attention and energy, and experimenting every day, has exploded my business, enriched my relationships, given me endless energy and passion, and even gotten my taxes done on time.

If you would like more support on this journey, please visit me at www.markjsilverman.com for information on how to work with me, or listen to the Mastering Midlife Podcast for the continued conversation.

In gratitude,

Mark J. Silverman

You can find Mark at
   Facebook: https://www.facebook.com/mark.silverman.54
   Instagram: @markjsilverman
   Linkedin: https://www.linkedin.com/in/mark22102/
   Twitter: @mjaysilverman and @masteringmidlif

ACKNOWLEDGEMENTS

A lifetime of friends, mentors and guides go into making a man who he is. I have been fortunate enough to have an unfair share of the world's gold standard.

Alan Cohen – I read *Relax into Wealth*, and everything changed. We talked, and you said you "had a hunch about me," which put me on the path I have been searching for my entire life. I met you in Hawaii and found my heart and my home. Nothing in my life would be as it is if I hadn't met you, and I am head over heels in love with my life. Thank you.

Rich Litvin – You have been the diamond cutter in my life. I brought 25 years of study, growth, and experience to our first conversation, and from that first connection you held the bar high. Sometimes so high I couldn't even see it, but you were unwavering in your belief that it was barely a stretch for me. Your wisdom, example, and love are invaluable to me finding my compass. Your silence, my foil. You are easily the best among the great. P.S. Without that one provocative question, this book would not exist.

Tom Mendoza – After I met you in Lanai, our mutual friend and colleague, Mike O. said, "The good news is, Tom Mendoza knows who you are. The bad news is, Tom Mendoza knows who you are, go sell something." It was never bad news. You are the leader I measure all others by. You taught me how to conduct myself in business with class and integrity and still win. I keep my "Top 10 Things I Learned from Tom Mendoza List" on hand to share with others.

Stan Bromley – Stan, I was a 30 year old waiter working my way through school (still). You took a chance on me and hired me into a professional position at the Four Seasons, even though I did not have the experience. It was the first time I had seen a fax machine (or worn a double breasted suit). You mentored me, believed in me, and showed me the first rungs on the ladder when I never even knew there was a ladder. Thank you, Sir.

Steve Chandler – I picked up *Time Warrior* and all my excuses went down like dominoes. We had one of the roughest conversations of my life, and it redoubled my resolve to succeed. I have read and listened to your wisdom so much that your voice is in my head daily helping me blow through any obstacle I momentarily think impossible. More importantly, your dedication to service in life and as a coach is my shining example of what is invaluable in this profession.

Michael Anderson – You are gifted at what you do and without a doubt, one of the most sound and grounded men I have met in my travels. You helped turn absolute hell into a life I could not imagine. I am forever grateful. P.S. You can cancel the Ritalin prescription.

Greg Collins – From the day I opened the door that you and Mike slammed in my face, you have had my back. Outstanding positions, giant commission checks, and awards did not compare with knowing I had your respect in the most competitive game in town. You are one of a kind, and one of my favorite people walking the planet.

ACKNOWLEDGEMENTS FOR
ONLY 10s 2.0

Tony, Helen, Christina, Katie and Jen – My Posse. My Foundation. Having you in my corner has moved me through crippling self-doubt and nearly impossible resistance to create more than I ever dreamed of. I cherish your friendship and your tough, on point, professional guidance.

Toby, Kate, Patti, Iris, Dawn, and Brady – You are the scaffolding that makes sense of everything this ADD brain creates. I have no idea how any of my work would get out to the world without your expertise and unshakable belief in me. Thank you for sharing your immense talent with me every day.

My Disruption and Innovation Club Partners Aliya, Vadym, Khy and Jeff – Thank you for adding laughter and edge to everything I do. You have helped this introvert find creative and fun ways to teach very deep and profound concepts.

Sean, Rob, Gorgio, Jonas, Al, Kate, Sarah, Jon, Dave, Guy, Bill, Ben, Rich, Steve, Mayosha, Tim, Ryan, Joe, John, and Jen – my clients and workshop attendees. Thank you for your trust. I am in awe of you and what you create in the world. I am better after each conversation.

Steve Hardison – I keep a picture of you and I on my altar. It is there to remind me who and what I could be in each moment.

Thank you for being that point of light. I have created "a life worth living."

The Bonnici Family – Tears stream down my cheeks as I try to write. My acknowledgement here has no words. Profound gratitude.

Dr. Christopher Ogilvie – Over a decade ago I walked into your office tired, in pain, and with a brain filled with fog. In eight weeks you healed me with your expertise, guidance, and extreme care. I walked out of your office thinking, "I'd like to do what he does, but I don't have any skills (medical or otherwise). I'd like to heal people." My life, my career, and everything I have done since then is from your example. Thank you for your friendship .

Patti M. Hall – You were the missing piece. This book, in its current form, and everything I write for the rest of my life, is your ripple.

A BIT ABOUT ME

This section is where an editor reads over my resume and writes a few paragraphs about how successful and influential I've been. Written well, these words should convince you that I have the credibility to offer insight and advice. But, since this is my book, I get to introduce myself to you the way I would like to.

A CEO who was evaluating whether to hire me to coach a couple of superstars on his team said to me, "Okay, Silverman. What's your deal?"

"Well," I said, "when I was 27, I rolled into Washington DC homeless and living in my truck, got sober, went to school and eight years later I was a millionaire, had two kids, and I was driving a Lexus convertible. Basically, I am a short, Jewish, Tony Robbins. What else would you like to know?"

I'll share with you that I couldn't believe what came out of my own mouth. He hired me on the spot.

And it was all true. In 1989 I was fortunate enough to have a wake up call and start my life in earnest. I got my college degree working as a waiter. I was married, (now divorced and remarried) with two incredible sons, Zack and Jake. I faced my fear every day and became successful in the tech startup world as a salesman eventually generating over $90 million in sales, and receiving numerous awards over the 15 years I spent at fast-moving, fast-growing companies like NetApp, VMware, EMC, and ServiceNow. I learned leadership in real time by leading teams to work with

CEOs, management, and front line stakeholders to bring mutual success and close multi-million deals.

My credibility is in my life. I have succeeded and failed more times than I can count both personally and professionally.

In my current role as coach, author, podcaster, and speaker – basically someone sharing experience and transformation – I have trained with some of the most profound teachers, coaches, and shamans in the world. I have spent 100s of thousands of dollars to learn leadership, relationship, spirituality, and possibility.

Everything I teach or share comes from the love I have for you. If a word or deed of mine makes a difference in your world, I am dedicated to bringing it to you.

ABOUT THE AUTHOR

Mark Silverman is a force of nature. When people spend time with him, they transform. Always. Some people aren't ready for it. The rare ones are, and they want more.

They are ready for an extraordinary life.

They are ready for an extraordinary business.

They are ready for an extraordinary relationship.

Mark is not a coach or a consultant, although he has coaching and consulting clients alike. Every engagement is unique.

The common thread is a leap forward towards the intended result.

Mark is very human, very honest, and very vulnerable. These qualities allow him to be real with his clients, and meet them on a deeper level than they are accustomed to, fostering long-lasting, exponential results.

Mark has generated over $90 million in sales, and received numerous awards over his 15-year career at fast-moving, fast-growing companies like NetApp, Vmware, and EMC. He has led teams to work with CEOs, management and front line stakeholders to bring mutual success and close multi-million deals. His dedication to the success of all involved, through leadership, coaching, and mentorship was the training ground for his passion to support others to achieve their goals.

He has also stumbled. Mark has experienced failure at a few business ventures and relationships along the way, and knows the lows that come with living a full-out life. He is a master at turning a challenging situation into gold.

If you're ready for something truly extraordinary, if you have a challenge, a project or a goal that needs a little rocket fuel ... or if you just know there is something more, but are not quite sure what it is, go to www.markjsilverman.com to find out how to work with Mark one-on-one. The only risk is getting what you want.

Made in United States
North Haven, CT
12 July 2022

21267330R00080